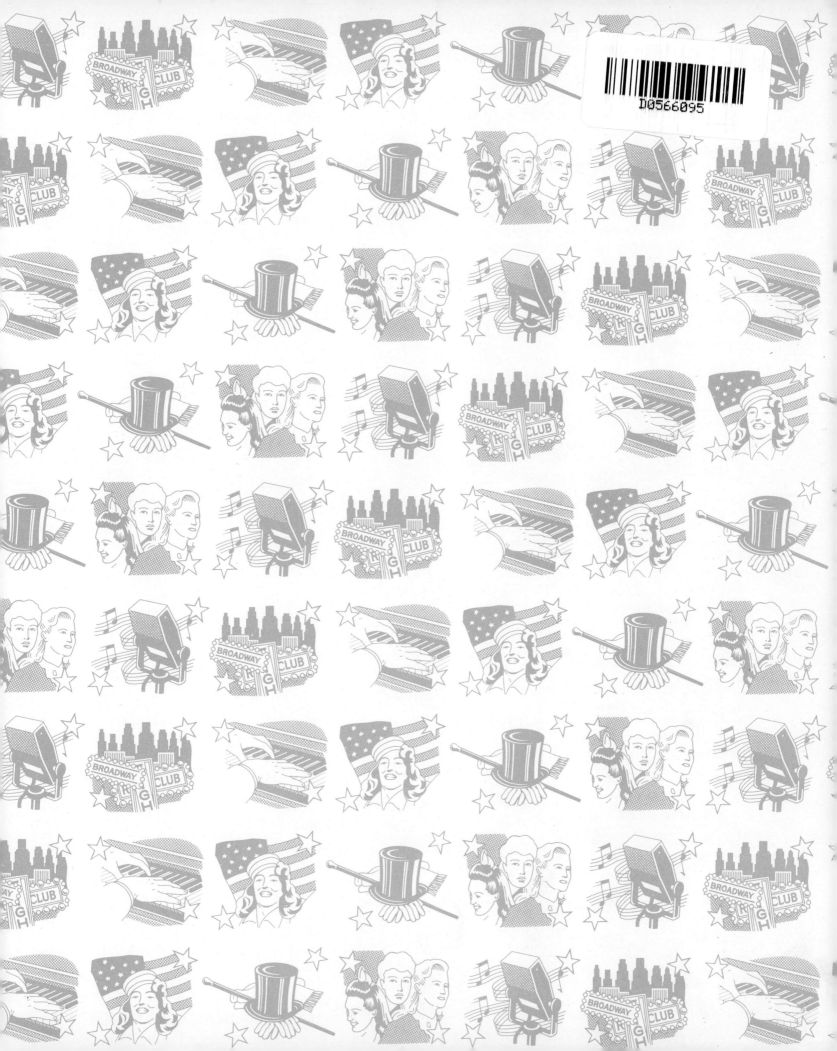

GLAMOROUS
☆ MUSICALS ☆

Ronald Bergan
GLAMOROUS MUSICALS
Fifty Years of Hollywood's Ultimate Fantasy

PEERAGE BOOKS

First Published in 1984
by Octopus Books Limited
59 Grosvenor Street
London W1

Second impression 1985

© 1984 Octopus Books Limited

ISBN 0 7064 2037 3

Produced by Mandarin Publishers
22a Westlands Road, Quarry Bay
Hong Kong

Printed in Hong Kong

Photographs supplied by
Joel W Finler

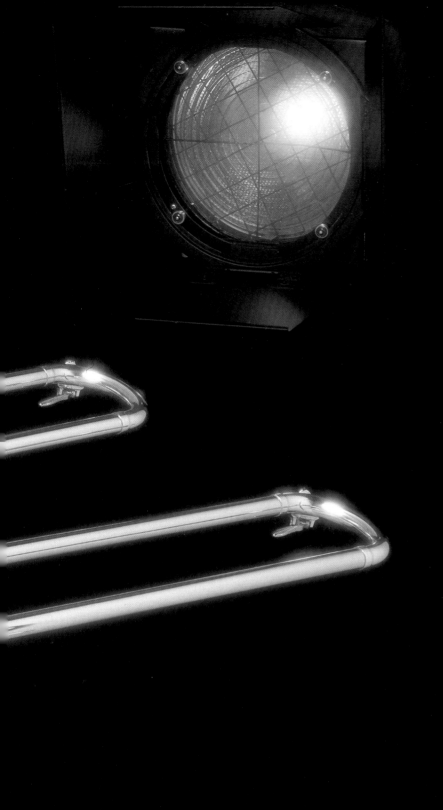

CONTENTS

Foreword by Ginger Rogers	6
Preface	8
THE EUROPEAN TOUCH	10
Marlene Dietrich	24
GLORIFYING THE AMERICAN GIRL	32
Al Jolson	43
THE LIGHT FANTASTIC	56
The Crooners	72
GENTLEMEN PREFER BLONDES	82
Marilyn Monroe	94
THAT'S ENTERTAINMENT	108
Black Stars	116
Cedric Gibbons	128
BROADWAY MELODIES	134
Hays Code	145
INDEX	158

FOREWORD

There was a time when the motion picture business was providing entertainment with a capital E; when wearing glamorous clothes in a movie was not unique – it was normal and expected by audiences. Today there's a reversal of those values of yesteryear. I am indeed proud and grateful that I was part of 'The Golden Age' of the film industry. Most of the musical films of that time gave audiences no problems to solve, only to sit back and hear famous composers and lyricists at their best. Writers wrote dialogue that sparkled of wit and humour. Having happy dialogue to speak and songs to sing that we knew would become standards, was a thrill never to be forgotten! 'Big screen and music' was a boon to theatre owners. We loved making those films, that's why they came forth so successfully. Artists designed magical sets for us to perform in, sets which were breathtaking to behold! This transported an audience into another world.

Designers of costumes had a field day. I've had the privilege of working with the best – minus one, Adrian. I regret not having had the opportunity to parade in some of his classic designs. Since I've always been clothes conscious, I've designed quite a few of my own costumes – or suggested to the couturier my taste. One gown, the gold lamé worn in the opening of *The Barkleys Of Broadway*, I designed. It worked well in 'The Swing Trot' number Astaire and I danced. Unfortunately the number was used under the credits and never really got the attention it should have. The dress added to the quick movements of the number but unless you read the credits, the dress and dance were missed. In *Lady In The Dark* I wore an Edith Head design, a mink skirt circular cut with solid beads under the circle plus a bodice of solid beads and rhinestones. The dress must have weighed over thirty pounds. When I had to perform the 'Jenny' number in this weighty gown, little did I know that I had to stand on a hemp rug to perform in it. With each step my stiletto heels were slipping through the hemp to constantly unbalance me. One may ask, 'Why didn't you stop and demand a removal of the hemp rug?' The answer to that is, – that I understand the producers' problem of forward movement on a tight production schedule where fifty extras are involved in a musical number. But *c'est la vie*, 'tis on film – no undoing it now!

Work has always excited me. The heavy schedules of dance in the RKO musicals were demanding; however, I've never been sorry for the gruelling hours spent in rehearsal halls five to six weeks prior to principal photography. Then came the six weeks of filming – but as I started my career as a dancer, dancing to me is representative of one of the highest expressions of joy. How could it have been otherwise working in ten musical films with the extremely versatile and talented Fred Astaire? To me our teaming – which was an unplanned association – was unquestionably a 'blessed event.'

This book's desire is to remind and refresh the joyous memories of the glamorous days of musical films. So, sit back and sing the songs as you read of the rainbows of yesterday.

PREFACE

If glamour is defined as magic, enchantment, beauty, charm, allurement, and sex appeal, then the screen musical is synonymous with glamour. The title of this book is, in a sense, tautological. Glamorous musicals are the rule not the exception, a condition that few ever wish to see altered. Born during the worst depression in modern times, the musical provided America with an immediate and accessible escape route. It was a magic carpet that took people instantly away from the bread-lines, dole queues, and the forgotten men and women. The movie musical extravaganza offered a panacea in the post-Depression years, was the opium of the people through the bitter period of World War II, and continued to waft the public away from harsh reality throughout the following decades. Even when it has treated less than glamorous subjects, the musical's intrinsic artificiality has somehow stripped them of pain. This Midas medium turns everything to gold. The essential, secret ingredient that has made the musical such a soothing balm to generations of filmgoers is, undoubtedly, glamour.

No other genre lends itself so easily to the creation of a never-never land, free from the restrictions that govern our normal daily lives – a country whose national anthem is 'There's No Business Like Show Business', whose temples are ornate theatres and sumptuous nightclubs where singing and dancing are the life-giving forces, and orchestras, invisible or otherwise, are everywhere. Judy Garland, in *The Pirate*, says 'I know there is a real world and a dream world and I shan't confuse them.' Ironically, this is precisely what the musical, as a whole, sets out to do. 'The cinema is a dream we all dream at the same time', Cocteau stated, and musicals, with their production numbers, are dreams within dreams. It is this unreality that has given directors, cameramen, and designers most creative scope within the commercial structure of Hollywood. With experiments in colour, the use of overhead shots, *trompe l'oeil*, split-screen techniques, superimposition, trick photography, surreal settings, animation, and juggling with time and space, the musical has been an important force in imaginative film-making, without being accused of 'avant-gardism' by cautious studio moguls.

Musicals could also, more easily, circumvent the censorious Hays Code, which far outreached Moses with its long list of Thou Shalt Nots. One of these was that 'Dancing in general is recognised as an art and as a beautiful form of expressing human emotions. But dances which suggest or represent sexual actions, whether performed solo or with two or more; dances intended to excite the emotional

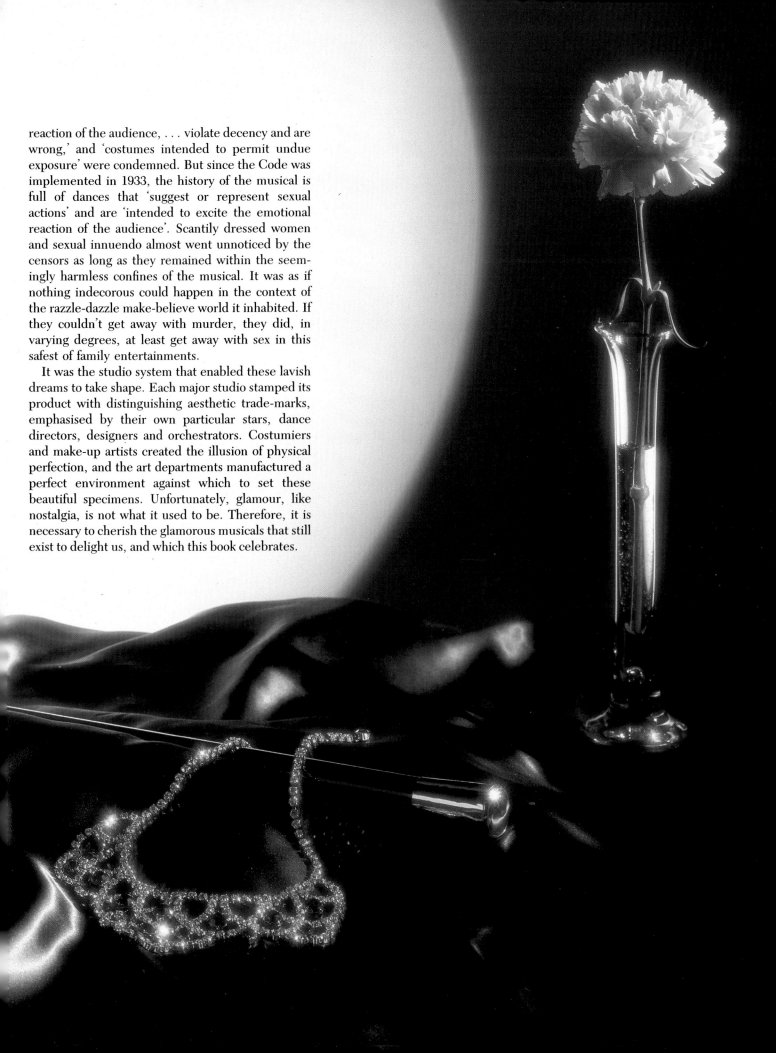

reaction of the audience, . . . violate decency and are wrong,' and 'costumes intended to permit undue exposure' were condemned. But since the Code was implemented in 1933, the history of the musical is full of dances that 'suggest or represent sexual actions' and are 'intended to excite the emotional reaction of the audience'. Scantily dressed women and sexual innuendo almost went unnoticed by the censors as long as they remained within the seemingly harmless confines of the musical. It was as if nothing indecorous could happen in the context of the razzle-dazzle make-believe world it inhabited. If they couldn't get away with murder, they did, in varying degrees, at least get away with sex in this safest of family entertainments.

It was the studio system that enabled these lavish dreams to take shape. Each major studio stamped its product with distinguishing aesthetic trade-marks, emphasised by their own particular stars, dance directors, designers and orchestrators. Costumiers and make-up artists created the illusion of physical perfection, and the art departments manufactured a perfect environment against which to set these beautiful specimens. Unfortunately, glamour, like nostalgia, is not what it used to be. Therefore, it is necessary to cherish the glamorous musicals that still exist to delight us, and which this book celebrates.

ABOVE *Lana Turner in* The Merry Widow (*MGM 1952*)   RIGHT *Tenor Mario Lanza and buxom soprano Kathryn Grayson*

THE EUROPEAN TOUCH

Paris loves lovers,
For lovers it's heaven above,
Paris tells lovers
'Love is supreme,
Wake up your dream,
And make love!'

Lyrics by Cole Porter
Sung by Fred Astaire
in *Silk Stockings* (1957)

The Hollywood musical reigned supreme in the consciously ironic misalliance between fantasy and reality. Hollywood dreamt Europe as a magical, mystical, phantasmagorical world, where the intoxicating fragrance of French-perfumed decor did not completely disguise the tantalising odour of depravity.

Since the earliest days of the cinema, Hollywood has portrayed Europe as a romantic wonderland in which France consisted of Paris, The Riviera, and the Casino at Monte Carlo; Italy was either Venice or an unspecified mountain town at Carnival time; Germany was a beer-quaffing Heidelberg, and Austria was the Tyrol, all whipped cream and waltzes – countries hardly distinguishable from the fanciful Marshovia, Romanza or Ruritania of operetta. Europe was a vast playground where American tourists would learn about *L'Amour* and *Savoir Vivre* from the worldly natives. Europe was wittier, sexier, more refined and, above all, more glamorous than America.

This vision was conjured up most potently in the Hollywood musical, which presented a Europe without poverty, fear or misery. Titian-haired soprano Jeanette MacDonald, the empress of screen operetta, waved and sang to happy peasants in the fields as she sped along in the Blue Express towards *Monte Carlo* (1930); and gorgeous damsels clustered at every window as French charmer Maurice Chevalier led his regiment through the streets singing 'Girls, Girls, Girls' in *The Merry Widow* (1934).

The capital of this mythical musical millennium was Paris, the Celestial City. But when the Germans goose-stepped to the

Arch of Triumph in 1940, the singing, dancing and kissing had to stop. It was as if Hollywood had been awakened from an amorous dream, only to find itself in the arms of a crone. During the war, the city was out of bounds to musicals. In peace, Paris reappeared in the musical with its charm intact. It had not been damaged by bombs, so all the well-loved landmarks remained to be reconstructed by the film studios' art departments. Once again, Paris meant elegant men and women drinking at Boulevard cafés, the Can-Can at the Moulin Rouge, and the gaiety of the Beaux Arts Ball. A city where Gene Kelly, *An American In Paris* (1951), could serenade Leslie Caron in the softly-Technicolored mists on the banks of the Seine; and Fred Astaire could convince Cyd Charisse in *Silk Stockings* (1957) that 'Paris Loves Lovers.'

In the late 20s and early 30s, artists and technicians from the studios of Europe flooded into Hollywood, bringing with them a cosmopolitan style and approach. The music-theatre background of these 'strangers in Paradise' was opera and operetta, usually set in a fantasy world of magic, gods and royalty, divorced from contemporary life. They did not perceive America as a glamorous enough setting for musical comedy, and knew little of the American tradition of vaudeville, the inspiration behind so many 'backstage' musicals. In America, girls were golddiggers or dames, in France they were courtesans or coquettes. America was bourbon, Europe was champagne. The emigrés themselves enjoyed perpetuating the image, and directors, designers and cameramen were given free rein to create this world of romance. Paramount was the most European of the studios in the 30s, its mountain logo symbolising the upper crust. It was the Cartier of studios, producing diamonds as big as the Ritz. Hans Dreier was the supervisory art director whose set designs established the lustrous surface that dictated the feel of the films. Leading cameramen like Victor Milner were masters in the diffusion of warm light in which radiant beauties, dressed in shimmering gowns by Travis Banton, could bathe. The decor of brocaded tapestries, revealing mirrors, voluptuous four-poster beds in vast ornamental bedrooms, cavernous halls with wide, ever-mounting staircases and ballrooms overhung with chandeliers was perfectly suited to the often risqué themes that were characteristic of the studio before The Hays Code scissors started its process of emasculation.

Ernst Lubitsch was the spirit of Paramount. Born in Berlin in 1892, he came to Hollywood in 1923. This *bon viveur* with the inappropriate forename brought

RIGHT *Lolo, Dodo, Jou-Jou, Clo-Clo, Margot and Frou-Frou, the gorgeous girls of Maxim's, falling prey to the charms of playboy Prince Danilo (Maurice Chevalier) in* The Merry Widow *(MGM 1934), directed by Ernst Lubitsch, the masterful purveyor of Continental sophistication and froth.*

LEFT *Jeanette MacDonald as Countess Helene Mara in Ernst Lubitsch's* Monte Carlo *(Paramount 1930) waking up ecstatically with a song on her lips from a Hans Dreier-designed bed, almost a cathedral of luxury.*

BELOW *Haughty and naughty soprano Jeanette MacDonald in one of her many wide-brimmed hats, and the look that prompted Maurice Chevalier to say in* The Merry Widow *(MGM 1934), 'Your right eye says yes, and your left eye says no.'*

13

ABOVE *Count Alfred Renard (Chevalier) gleefully wooing Queen Louise (MacDonald) in Lubitsch's* The Love Parade *(1929), the setting is a typically lavish boudoir, one of those salons of seduction around which many Paramount operettas revolved.*

RIGHT *Anglo-Saxon Jeanette MacDonald and 'Latin Lover' Ramon Novarro embrace in* The Cat And The Fiddle *(MGM 1934), a stylish and suggestive musical. Novarro, the romantic Mexican-born star, was brutally murdered in his Hollywood home in 1968.*
OPPOSITE *The sultry Pola Negri as Catherine the Great with director Ernst Lubitsch on the set of* Forbidden Paradise *(Paramount 1924), one of many ironic costume films they made together, a vein which Lubitsch continued in his musicals. Negri reputedly had a love affair with Valentino.*

14

continental manners and hedonism into puritan America, kissing the public's hand with sophistication. The famous 'Lubitsch touch' has been variously defined, but the touch is that of a master chef who knows exactly the right amount of spice or sugar to add to a dish. He had the extraordinary ability to hint at what went on behind closed doors. 'I let the audience use their imaginations. Can I help it if they misconstrue my suggestions?' he remarked mischievously. Paris was the glittering backdrop for the three musicals he directed starring Jeanette MacDonald and Maurice Chevalier. 'I've been to Paris, France, but Paris, Paramount is better' Lubitsch once admitted.

Chevalier was over forty when he made his

Hollywood debut in the first of them, *Innocents In Paris* (1929), but with his straw hat perched at a roguish angle, his jutting lower lip expectant of a kiss, and a French accent as broad as the Champs Elysees, he epitomised the sexually confident, Parisian boulevardier. He could make the simplest song or line sound suggestive. His gallic charm and Jeanette MacDonald's Anglo-Saxon reserve and self-mockery produced a seductive, piquant combination. She made her entrance into motion pictures in *The Love Parade* (1929), Lubitsch's first talkie. He immediately realised that the camera and sound effects could be used with greater flexibility than hitherto in order to counterpoint the musical scenes. This saucy fairy tale is set in Paris and the fictional land of Sylvania of which Jeanette MacDonald is Queen. Dressed in a diaphanous nightdress, designed by Travis Banton, she awakens in the royal bedchamber singing of her 'Dream Lover', attended by four ladies-in-waiting. The lover materialises in the shape of Chevalier as Count Alfred Renard who woos her in the strangest manner by comparing her to all his former conquests in 'My Love Parade'. He soon becomes her Prince Consort, but is only happy when she makes him her King and master. With its lavish settings, songs integrated into the scenario and sexual innuendo, *The Love Parade* set the pattern for screen operettas.

Lubitsch then directed MacDonald and Chevalier separately before teaming them up again. In *Monte Carlo*, she is a Countess fleeing to the south of France on her wedding night, wearing only lingerie under her coat. There she meets Jack Buchanan as a Count posing as a hairdresser to be near her. The film is less lewd than its predecessor, thanks to Buchanan's rather weedy, English elegance. In the musical numbers, Lubitsch again breaks new ground. As a train picks up speed on its way to Monte Carlo, MacDonald sings 'Beyond The Blue Horizon' with her hair blowing in the breeze, the music syncopated with the sound of the locomotive. 'Give Me A Moment, Please' is a love duet sung over the telephone; the camera follows the couple on their separate ways to the Casino as they sing 'Always In All Ways'. Maurice Chevalier is *The Smiling Lieutenant* (1931), flanked by demi-mondaine Claudette Colbert and Miriam Hopkins as his Princess wife. Though Colbert is having an affair with Chevalier, she decides to help Hopkins save her marriage by advising her to 'Jazz Up Your Lingerie'. With assistance from the superb Paramount make-up and costume department, Hopkins is transformed into a desirable enough lady to keep her officer husband home nights. Lubitsch pokes sly fun at the antics of his European aristocrats, but concurs

'*The love-making which I like is that with the light touch of humour, the smile, but yet sincere. None of this romantic stuff, with everything so serious. I do not feel comfortable in that kind of role. It is not my type. Love, with a bit of humour, is what they like in Paris.*'

Maurice Chevalier in 1930

RIGHT *Princess Jeanette MacDonald being measured by tailor Maurice Chevalier in the boudoir of her château, in Rouben Mamoulian's* Love Me Tonight *(Paramount 1932), another excuse to get Jeanette to reveal her physical attributes at this period.*
OPPOSITE *Chevalier the tailor, pretending to be a Baron, entertains fellow-guests at an elaborate costume ball in* Love Me Tonight *(Paramount 1932), by recounting the story of 'The Poor Apache', using shadows on the wall and bringing earthiness to the refined atmosphere.*
BELOW *Leonard Hall, writing in* Photoplay 1931 *on Jeanette MacDonald.*

HERR Lubitsch – the tamer of Pola Negri – was looking for a leading woman for this French meteor, Chevalier. The picture (*Love Parade*) was to be gay, frothy, phony-kingdom business. He'd tried girl after girl, and it was no dice. He saw something in the singing talking shadow of a beautiful girl with red-gold hair. His smart show business sense told him he could add to it – gaiety, finesse, and most important of all, glamour.

with the film's conclusion that beauty being skin deep is deep enough. MacDonald and Chevalier were reunited for *One Hour With You* (1932), partly directed by George Cukor, another frothy boudoir operetta about infidelity. Like the previous movie, the music was by Oscar Straus, including the title song performed at a party given in Chevalier's luxurious Parisian home. Much of the dialogue (by Samson Raphaelson) is in rhyming couplets such as 'Unless you're well mated, this business of marriage is much over-rated.' MacDonald as Chevalier's wife appears once more in revealing lingerie and Genevieve Tobin plays a vivacious vamp called Mitzi, in saucy hats to match her morality, of whom her husband remarks, 'When I married her she was a brunette, now you can't believe a word she says.'

Russian-born Rouben Mamoulian directed *Love Me Tonight* (1932), using the same team – Travis Banton (costumes), Hans Dreier (sets), Victor Milner (camera) – with MacDonald and Chevalier making their last Paramount film together. Witty, stylish, imaginative and cohesive, it is conceived entirely in musical terms. It opens with the sounds of Paris

waking up until the streets of The Latin Quarter are teeming with friendly, singing shopkeepers. One of them, the tailor (Chevalier), starts to hum 'Isn't It Romantic' in his shop. The tune is continued by a customer, overheard by a taxi-driver, a composer in the cab writes it down, he adds words to it on a train where it is picked up by soldiers who are seen singing it on the march. A gypsy hears it, plays it on his violin and Princess Jeanette on a balcony of her medieval château sings the melody thus linking her by this musical chain to Chevalier before they meet. Their first encounter takes place when she is whirling through the woods in her horse and carriage singing 'Lover' and his auto has broken down. He is taken for a Baron and installed in the château until the family discover that 'the son of a gun is nothing but a tailor.' Chevalier's love at first sight is expressed by the song 'Mimi' (although that is not her name), such a catchy refrain that the rest of the cast can't resist singing it. (When the film was brought back in 1950, Myrna Loy's rendition was cut because her navel was visible through her nightgown.) The love-sick Princess is visited by a doctor who can only say, 'with eyes and red lips and a figure like that, you're

not wasting away. You're just wasted.' It was the last time Banton was to dress that figure.

The other king of Hollywood costume design in the 30s was Adrian at MGM. Born Gilbert Adrian Greenburg in 1903, he became renowned as the creator of exquisite gowns for Hollywood's most legendary beauties, especially the luminous Greta Garbo. For *The Merry Widow*, Adrian created foundation garments for Jeanette MacDonald that reshaped her figure. While keeping the lines of the period dresses, he used light chiffon and voile so that she could move easily. With Sydney Guilaroff's hair styles and Oliver T. Marsh's high gloss photography, Jeanette MacDonald never looked lovelier. Lubitsch chose her against the wishes of Chevalier who, despite their three films together, did not get on with her (Chevalier wanted opera singer Grace Moore for the part. She even offered to do it for nothing, but at over 135 lbs, Lubitsch found her unsuitable). Lubitsch arrived at MGM, complete with his scriptwriters, Ernest Vajda and Samson Raphaelson, and a list of extravagant demands in set design. Cedric Gibbons, the supreme MGM art director, gave in to them, the film cost over a million dollars, and the Lubitsch touch remained intact. It looks every bit its cost, with Gibbons and his assistant Frederic Hope winning an Academy Award for Best Interior Decoration. (Incidentally, Gibbons was the designer of the Oscar statuette). The film moves from one wondrous moment to the next. 'Vilia' sung in shadow from a gypsy camp to MacDonald lit high on a balcony; her literal discarding of her widowhood by changing all her possessions from black mourning into dazzling white (even her black pekinese); a lyrical tracking shot

LEFT *Maurice Chevalier joining two Maxim's beauties in a Can-Can from Ernst Lubitsch's* The Merry Widow *(MGM 1934) at the famous cafe, synonymous with the gaiety and glamour of Paris, constantly recreated in Hollywood.*

ABOVE *Nonchalant Ernst Lubitsch (1892–1947), with his perpetual cigar – the man whose 'touch' established the Paramount studio style of elegance, wit and cynicism in opulent surroundings during the 30s.*

outside the separate apartments of the now merry widow and Chevalier as he sings of going to Maxim's; the champagne effervescence of that famed café, and the 'Merry Widow Waltz' finale, the dancers dressed in sharply contrasting black and white (costumed by Ali Hubert), whirling through a mirrored ballroom shot from above. It was, according to Andrew Sarris, 'the last musical of a certain spirit and style to be made on this planet.'

Lubitsch only returned to the musical fourteen years later with *That Lady In Ermine* (1948) for Fox, an attempt at Ruritania Regained. However, his health,

the world and the cinema had altered much in the interim and he shot eight days of the film before dying of a heart attack on November 30th, 1947. (It was completed by the Viennese director Otto Preminger). This lumpish Technicolor fantasy-romance, tells of the love of a hussar (Douglas Fairbanks Jr) for a beautiful countess (Betty Grable). The plot shifts from 1561 to 1861, so it was a challenge for dress designers Rene Hubert and Charles Le Maire to give Grable sufficient opportunity to display her famous legs. As much of it takes place in the hussar's dreams, they managed to design an enormous transparent white

She makes history-in the musical that's laughter, splendour and romance!

BETTY GRABLE · DOUGLAS FAIRBANKS Jr.

That LADY IN ERMINE

COLOR BY TECHNICOLOR

CESAR ROMERO
WALTER ABEL · REGINALD GARDINER

ERNST LUBITSCH

20 CENTURY-FOX

ABOVE *Although* That Lady In Ermine *(1948) was set in the Hungary of 1561 and 1861, Twentieth Century-Fox's publicists made sure that Betty Grable's 'million dollar legs' were well on display (four times!) in this typically eye-catching poster of the 40s.*

chiffon hooped skirt that flew up as she danced. The bland blonde played a double role and was miscast in both of them.

Austria was the romantic locale of *The Emperor Waltz* (1948), a homage paid to Lubitsch by one of his most distinguished disciples, Billy Wilder. Set in the Tyrol (but filmed in the Canadian Rockies) '40 years ago', the time of Wilder's birth in Austria, it presumed to capture the country of his youth. His first film in colour, he paid particular attention to every aspect of it, even having the daisies painted blue because 'white photographs too glaringly.' Edith Head, who designed most of Wilder's films at Paramount, made the ravishing dresses worn by Joan Fontaine as the niece of the Emperor Franz Josef. Although splendid on the eye, it turned out to be no more than a slightly better class of Bing Crosby musical. As if to emphasize the fact, MGM remade *The Merry Widow* (1952) in which Fernando Lamas, a languid Latin lover in tight pants, replaced the ebullient Chevalier; a non-singing, non-acting Lana Turner took over from Jeanette Mac-Donald, and gracelessness replaced charm. The European tradition was preserved to the letter, but the spirit was missing. True, there was a certain elegance in Helen Rose's costumes, but they lacked period authenticity. The chorus girls at Maxim's made up a brilliant show of scarlet and black, and in the waltz scene, the dancers wore pink, white and gold. Turner stood out in a richly embroidered black velvet gown flared above the knees with black egret feathers held against her blonde hair. But the era of the true cinematic operetta was long gone. Lubitsch was well and truly dead.

In the 30s, Paramount represented High Society,

RIGHT *Lana Turner in* The Merry Widow *(1952) with Fernando Lamas, MGM's Latin Lover who did his best in the role of Count Danilo but could not erase the glorious memory of Chevalier's gallic charm.*

Warner Bros. the working classes, and MGM was the studio that most reflected bourgeois values. When Paramount was naughty, MGM was nice. Paramount addressed itself to adults, MGM to the family. MGM had more money, more space and more stars than any other studio. It was a kingdom whose annual turnover was said to be three times that of Portugal. After *The Merry Widow* (1934), they continued the operetta tradition by teaming Jeanette MacDonald up with Nelson Eddy for eight lavish musicals. Most of them were produced by Hunt Stromberg, five were directed by W.S. Van Dyke, and the other three by Robert Z. Leonard; Cedric Gibbons was responsible for the grandiose sets (including a vast garret in Vienna in *Bitter Sweet*, 1940, where the couple are supposed to be living in poverty), Douglas Shearer (brother to Norma) the superb sound recording, William Daniels and Oliver T. Marsh captured them through the camera, and Adrian executed the clean-lined 'period'

LEFT *The kitschy 'Wooden Shoes' finale from* Sweethearts *(MGM 1938), with Jeanette MacDonald and Nelson Eddy. She is wearing a pink tuille, gold-sequined Dutch girl dress designed by Adrian, parodying his own earlier style.*

LEFT *Jeanette MacDonald as the diva Marie De Flor, brought glamour into the Canadian Wilds in* Rose Marie *(MGM 1936); here, she engages in the 'Indian Love Call' duet, with Nelson Eddy as a singing mountie.*

21

ABOVE *The two profiles of 'The Iron Butterfly' and 'The Singing Capon', Jeanette MacDonald and Nelson Eddy, coming together in* Sweethearts *(MGM 1938), she a mass of ruffles and bows provided by designer Adrian.*

costumes. The dance director was Albertina Rasch from Vienna whose speciality, described by Arlene Croce, 'was toe-dancers doing *relevé* in strict time and strict formation or fluttering in moth-like droves while the camera peered down from the flies.' The series was unashamedly sentimental, but it was extremely popular and brought much-needed glamour into an austere period. 'Today, anything that has a suggestion of sentiment is quickly dismissed as corn,' MacDonald explained in an interview in 1964. 'Frankly, what's wrong with it? Have we become so sufficient that we can live without sentiment? Sentiment, after all, is basic. Without it, there is no love, no life, no family.' And certainly no *Naughty Marietta* (1935), *Rose Marie* (1936), *Maytime* (1937), *The Girl Of The Golden West* (1938), *Sweethearts* (1938), *New Moon* (1940), *Bitter Sweet* (1940) and *I Married An Angel* (1942). As Lotte Eisner has pointed out, they are good examples of Hollywood kitsch, particularly *Maytime* with its

blossoming trees and sentimentalized bucolicism. In fact, there is something in the aryan qualities of MacDonald and Eddy which is not unlike the aesthetics of the escapist films produced in Nazi Germany at the same time.

Jeanette MacDonald, although in her mid to late thirties, continued to play the coquettish ingenue, on and off screen. She would instruct the cameraman to favour her left profile and hog all the best camera angles from her male partners. John Barrymore is reputed to have reacted to her scene-stealing on the set of *Maytime*, by shouting, 'If you wave that loathsome chiffon rag you call a kerchief once more while I'm speaking, I shall ram it down your gurgling throat!' In *Bitter Sweet*, she tried to convince as an 18-year-old English lass. Because of her elongated face and neck, Adrian designed wide-brimmed hats that were high off the face, wigs with masses of curls at the sides and elaborate high collars and chokers. However, with her long legs and no hips, he found her easy to dress in slim-lined Empire gowns. As she began to put on weight, Adrian disguised it with corsets and astute tailoring. *Sweethearts* introduced the couple into a contemporary setting for the first time. It was the first three-strip Technicolor film made by MGM, giving Adrian a chance to design gowns with colour in mind. Jeanette MacDonald was made a bright redhead for the picture but, despite the bright red hair and her green eyes, Adrian dressed her throughout the film in pale pink shades. In the title number, a gentle parody of operetta that takes place on stage, she wears a pink tuille and gold sequined dress, a comment on all the sequined dresses Adrian had made for her in the past.

Nelson Eddy was never comfortable in front of the camera, and the more animated MacDonald became, the more wooden he seemed. He was, in fact, the dumb blonde of the pair. W.S.. 'Woody' Van Dyke complained, 'I've handled Indians, African natives, South Sea Islanders, rhinos, pygmies and Eskimos and made them act – but not Nelson Eddy.' But he was handsome, looked good in a variety of uniforms, and his stolid baritone blended well with MacDonald's trilly soprano voice in duets such as 'Ah Sweet Mystery Of Life!', 'The Indian Love Call', and 'Lover Come Back To Me.' Some wag dubbed them, 'The Singing Capon and The Iron Butterfly.' After the failure of *I Married An Angel*, one of the most successful partnerships in motion picture history broke up without regrets. When MacDonald died in 1965, she left one thing to Eddy – a print of *Rose Marie*.

After three films with Eddy, Jeanette MacDonald begged Louis B. Mayer to allow her to make one

ABOVE *In the costumes of 19th-century Spain, MacDonald played the title role of* The Firefly *(MGM 1937); here, she imperiously greets handsome tenor Allan Jones (right) while George Zucco looks on.*

without him. The result was the no-expenses spared *The Firefly* (1937). Although the Verona square of the previous year's *Romeo And Juliet* was redecorated to represent the Madrid of 1808, it was only one of thirty major sets. Cedric Gibbons and his set decorators made special trips to Europe to buy props and costume materials. Adrian and his staff designed 1,700 special costumes plus fourteen ensembles for MacDonald. She took dancing lessons in the bolero and flamenco from Albertina Rasch for her role as Nina Maria Azara, the Firefly of the title, a spy posing as a café dancer. For one sequence in which she is seen dancing on a table top, Oliver Marsh had a camera revolve above her at 360 degrees so she appeared to be spinning at incredible speed. Her handsome partner was curly-haired tenor Allan Jones, whose unavailability for *Naughty Marietta* had gained Nelson Eddy the part. He sang the hit song 'The Donkey Serenade' to MacDonald as they rode clop-clop by coach over the Spanish mountains. It was directed by Robert Z. Leonard at the same pace.

Meanwhile, Nelson Eddy was paired with the sublimely leggy dancer Eleanor Powell in the preposterous *Rosalie* (1937), a kitschy cross between an operetta and a college campus musical, the first half taking place in America where Eddy is a West Point cadet and Powell is the Princess of Romanza studying at Vassar. The title song (hated by its composer, Cole Porter) is first sung by Eddy beneath her dormitory window and reprised in Romanza by Powell, in a frothy tutu and pom-poms, and a cast of thousands

including the Albertina Rasch Dancers clad in scanty slave-girl outfits designed by Dolly Tree.

The era of MGM's opulent operettas neared its end with *The Great Waltz* (1938) or 'The Great Schmaltz', a highly fictionalised and sentimental biopic on the life of Johann Strauss. However, it gave ample opportunity for Cedric Gibbons to recreate the ballrooms and biergartens of late 19th-century Vienna, and to Albertina Rasch to fill them with waltzing couples dressed by Adrian in expensive laces and silks. Adrian had a particular liking for large bows stretched across the shoulders. 'Whenever Adrian has a problem with some part of the costume, he sticks a bow over it,'

LEFT *The pulchritudinous under-graduates at Vassar, in embroidered silk pyjamas, watching Eleanor Powell (as the Princess of Romanza) tap dance through the college dormitory to 'I've A Strange New Rhythm In My Heart' from* Rosalie *(MGM 1937).*

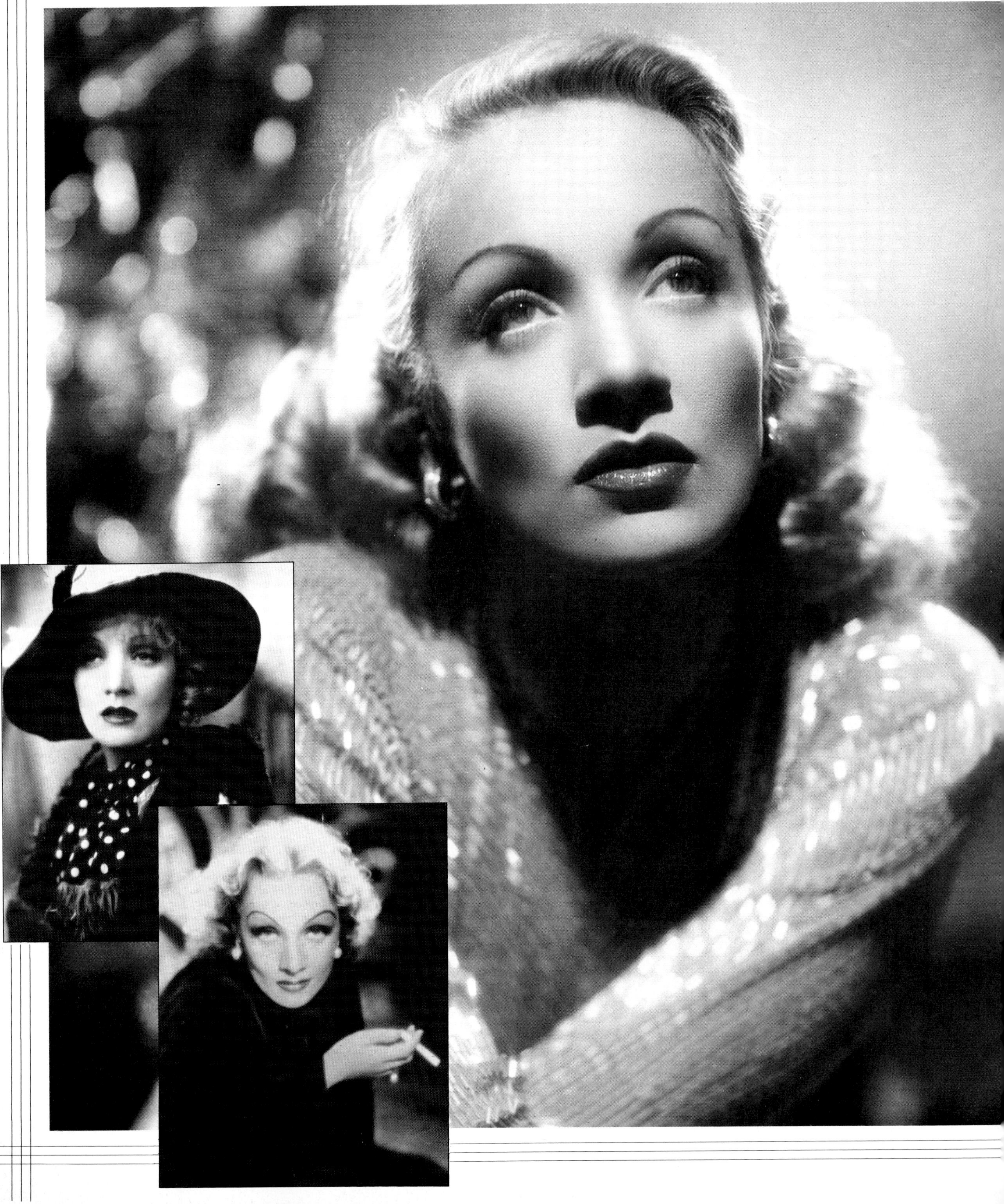

MARLENE DIETRICH

No movie in which Marlene Dietrich appeared was a complete musical, but her presence lent them all a kind of music. Since *The Blue Angel*, her seductive languor promised that, any moment, she might arrange her body as though for love, and husk 'Falling In Love Again...' Hers was a pillow-talk voice of the kind that men might dream to hear.

She belonged to the European look fostered by Paramount and inherent in the Lubitsch-style sophistication. In her world, there was an understanding that women were not merely demure objects of men's desire. She was the kind of woman who would love back after making the initial overtures. And then, beware! She was, to all men, a seductress. But to women there was, within her public image, a certain sense of her sexual ambiguity, and her off-screen appearances in stylishly masculine trousers influenced a whole generation.

She could mock her voice's reach and range as in 'See What The Boys In The Backroom Will Have' in *Destry Rides Again*, and yet that same vocal instrument could pierce the heart with 'Where Have All The Flowers Gone?' It was in truth a voice for cabaret. It came, as she did, from the Berlin of Brecht and Weill. It was free of their comment, but not of cruelty.

INSET LEFT *Dietrich in Paramount's* Blonde Venus *(1932), the Von Sternberg film in which, playing a German café singer.*
BOTTOM INSET *The glamour of her sophistication and allure is evident in this archetypical portrait.*

BOTTOM *Marlene in* A Foreign Affair *(1948).*
BELOW *La Dietrich photographed during a ten-minute rest between takes on the set of* Desire *(1936), a romantic concoction from Lubitsch and Paramount.*

complained Luise Rainer who played Strauss's neglected wife. It was the other woman, Polish soprano Miliza Korjus who had all the best tunes and gowns. Typically, this most Viennese of subjects was given to French director Julian Duvivier, making his first Hollywood movie, and dapper Frenchman Fernand Gravet played Johann Strauss. In a delightfully absurd rhythmic sequence, we learn that Strauss composed the whole of his 'Tales From The Vienna Woods' while riding through the self-same woods, by taking the melodies from the birds.

In 1930, Metro Goldwyn Mayer brought the Metropolitan Opera's Grace Moore to Hollywood to play Jenny Lind, 'The Swedish Nightingale', in *A Lady's Morals*. After being turned down by MGM for *The Merry Widow*, she signed with Columbia where she scored her greatest triumph in *One Night Of Love* (1934). Somewhat mirroring her own career, it told of an American soprano who studies in Italy and wins fame at the Met. It was the first of five deliriously silly, well-mounted, tuneful operettas she made for Columbia. Harry Cohn, the head of the studio, would check all the costume sketches for his leading ladies to make sure they were in 'good taste'. Robert Kalloch, the first major designer to work for Columbia, dressed Grace

RIGHT *Gladys Swarthout, the alluring mezzo-soprano, brought to Hollywood in the 30s as a rival to Grace Moore and Jeanette MacDonald, in a scene from* Romance In The Dark *(Paramount 1938), one of the four florid operetta films in which she appeared.*

RIGHT *The notorious mistress of newspaper magnate William Randolph Hearst, Marion Davies (the only blonde in the Sextette), in the Gay Nineties musical* The Floradora Girl *(MGM 1930), displaying delicate prettiness and comic flair.*

LEFT *Universal's fresh-faced
juvenile soprano Deanna
Durbin, 'the ideal daughter
millions of fathers and mothers
wished they had', delighting high
society with her bell-like tones in*
One Hundred men And A Girl
(1937).

Moore to Cohn's satisfaction. Not surprisingly, she is at her most ravishing in *The King Steps Out* (1936), directed by Marlene Dietrich's Svengali, Joseph Von Sternberg, making his only true musical, a Viennese romance obviously influenced by Lubitsch. Grace Moore was killed in a plane crash on January 26th, 1947. Kathryn Grayson impersonated her in 1953 in *So This Is Love* (GB: *The Grace Moore Story*), a biopic that, typical of the genre, managed to ignore her tragic death. Moore was the first genuine prima donna to become a success in a Hollywood musical.

A fter *One Night Of Love*, operatic arias began to creep into more and more musicals. RKO quickly signed up French coloratura Lily Pons for three films in which she interrupted the low-brow proceedings with her high-pitched voice. Jeanette MacDonald first attempted opera in *San Francisco* (1936), literally bringing the house down with arias from 'Faust' and 'La Traviata'. In *Maytime*, she and Nelson Eddy are opera singers who realise they love each other while singing in a specially composed opera based on themes from Tchaikovsky's 5th symphony. The only real chance Eddy ever had to sing at the Met was in the form of a singing whale in Disney's *Make Mine Music* (1946). Parker Tyler suggests that it was somehow a 'satire on the bulk of opera singers in contrast to the charm of their voices.' Yet, the opera

house in movies has largely been used as a baroque background against which romantic trysts and intrigues take place, while snatches of arias rudely interrupt the dialogue of the bejewelled ladies and dinner-jacketed gentlemen in the loges. As Hollywood musicals have been an antidote to solemnity, 'high art' has generally been greeted with deep suspicion. The view that classical music can only be swallowed if the pill is sugared has led to some weird incongruities such as the famed dramatic soprano Kirsten Flagstad being introduced by Bob Hope in *The Big Broadcast of 1938*, conductor Leopold Stokowski meeting Mickey Mouse in *Fantasia* (1940), and Wagnerian tenor Lauritz Melchior in *Thrill Of Romance* (1945) coming face to face with glamorous swimming star Esther Williams.

The European touch was kept alive by emigré producers and directors, who spread their mittel-European sweetness and light into mittel-America. The most successful purveyor of popular classics was Hungarian-born producer Joe Pasternak. He had a penchant for nubile sopranos and was responsible for making Deanna Durbin, Kathryn Grayson, Jane Powell and Ann Blyth into stars. Durbin, a well-scrubbed Pollyanna, saved Universal Studios from bankruptcy. Pasternak steered 'The Watteau Shepherdess of Universal' through ten musicals in which she soothed world-weary adults with her bell-like voice. She reconciles her divorced parents in

BELOW *Lauritz Melchior, the
great Wagnerian helden tenor,
who brought a bit of culture,
sturdy singing, and good nature
to his appearances in five
Hollywood musicals, here giving
avuncular support to the
feminine fineries of Esther
Williams, Kathryn Grayson and
Jane Powell.*

ABOVE *Deanna Durbin, grown up and glamourized, in her only Technicolor feature,* Can't Help Singing *(1944), a period musical on which Universal lavished more money than on previous Durbin vehicles.*

BELOW *Diminutive, lilting lyric soprano Ann Blyth as the irresistible barmaid to the beer-quaffing Heidelberg students in Sigmund Romberg's* The Student Prince *(MGM 1954), one of the last of the screen operettas.*

Three Smart Girls (1936), she marries off her sisters in *Three Smart Girls Grow Up* (1938) and she charms Leopold Stokowski into conducting her father's orchestra of unemployed musicians in *100 Men And A Girl* (1937). When asked by the Maestro what she has chosen to sing with the orchestra, she *merely* replies 'Traviata'. Durbin was the ideal teenager, whose modestly cut dresses (by Vera West) were imitated by young girls at every college dance throughout the country. Her popularity in Europe is poignantly demonstrated by her photo, cut from a movie magazine, that was found above Anne Frank's bed in the secret attic in Amsterdam where the young diarist hid from the Nazis.

Pasternak deserted her in 1942 in order to go to MGM so, at the age of 21, her career faltered. Adrian was brought in to add sophistication to her image in *Hers To Hold* (1943) and *His Butler's Sister* (1943), but she refused to trim down her figure. Indeed, Walter Plunkett who designed the period dresses for her only colour film, *Can't Help Singing* (1944), recalls saying to her, 'Dear, aren't you getting a bit heavy?' Deanna replied, 'It doesn't matter, dear, you can always let my dresses out at the sides.' For the finale of this costume musical set in the west in 1847, Durbin couldn't decide which of two dresses she would wear. She ended up wearing both in the same sequence.

Meanwhile, Pasternak was getting his new protégée, Kathryn Grayson, to raise the cultural tone of such MGM musicals as *Thousands Cheer* (1943), *Anchors Aweigh* (1945), and *Two Sisters From Boston* (1946), the latter finding her singing at the Met with Lauritz Melchior (without a rehearsal) in a meaningless mish-mash of an opera based on themes by Mendelssohn and Liszt. Grayson's china-doll features, *retroussé* nose and shrill coloratura were matched with the beefy frame and strident tenor of Mario Lanza, Pasternak's latest discovery, in *That Midnight Kiss* (1949) and *The Toast of New Orleans* (1950). Mario Lanza was the most famous of all operatic singers in the movies, although his drugs-alcohol-food problems got as much publicity as his voice. His gluttony caused consternation among the costumiers who had to keep altering his clothes during shooting. Miss Grayson refused to work with him again because of his boorish behavior. Joseph Ruttenberg, the cinematographer on *The Great Caruso* (1951) commented, 'such bursts of ego, of self-inflation I have rarely seen on a movie set. He was a royal pain.' But Lanza's lusty singing and temperamental personality, almost a caricature of the Italian tenor, obviously had a wide appeal and *The Great Caruso* was one of MGM's biggest box-office hits. This wildly inaccurate, mawkish biopic, contained nine scenes from operas and dozens of arias. Ironically, the most successful song of the film was 'The Loveliest Night Of The Year' sung by Ann Blyth as Caruso's wife, while waltzing with her husband at an Italian restaurant in New York. Luckily for MGM, Lanza had recorded the songs for the CinamaScope production of *The Student Prince* (1954) before walking out on it. Thus, his voice is heard bellowing incongruously out of the slim frame of Edmund Purdom in this dated operetta about the love of a prince for a barmaid (Ann Blyth) in the Heidelberg of 1894. Mario Lanza died in Rome in October 1958 at the age of 38.

Petite, 17-year-old lyric soprano Jane Powell was perfect material through which Joe Pasternak could relive his days at Universal with Deanna Durbin. After two minor musicals for United Artists, she was

made into a blonde and put into Durbin's shoes as a teenage Miss Fixit in Technicolor rehashes of the earlier vehicles, with the usual musical mixture of the light and classical. Pasternak's favourite emblems of 'long-haired' music were Lauritz Melchior, and the Spanish virtuoso pianist, Jose Iturbi, who always appeared as himself. Both appeared regularly as musical mentors of Jane Powell and Kathryn Grayson. In *Holiday in Mexico* (1946), Powell has a crush on Iturbi, and in *Luxury Liner* (1948), she gets to sing a duet from Verdi's 'Aida' with Melchior. Jeanette MacDonald, as Powell's mother in *Three Daring Daughters* (1948), her penultimate film, actually marries Iturbi! Young Miss Powell warbled pleasantly through these glossy, gossamer entertainments, but had to wait until she was twenty-five before graduating to adulthood and her best role in *Seven Brides For Seven Brothers* (1954). In *Rich, Young and Pretty* (1951), she plays a Texan girl visiting Paris and meeting her mother (Danielle Darrieux), a lady who had deserted her husband many years before for the more sophisticated life of Europe.

Paris once more became a luminous cinema beacon in the 50s, the ideal backdrop for romance. Musicals set in The City of Light were again as much 'oo-la-la' as 'tra-la-la'. But Paris was also the home of *haute couture*. A visit to a fashion house in Paris is as much on the middle-class American tourist's agenda as the Louvre, and to own a Paris gown is the height of luxury. As most costumes worn in Hollywood movies were specially designed by top couturiers, a fashion parade within a musical seems rather *de trop*. But Fred Astaire announces during the fashion show finale of *Roberta* (1935), 'We'll show you the gown we made for Marie, Queen of Roumania. We also ran up three of these for Mrs Sludge of Pennsylvania.' What the Mrs Sludges in the cinema audience watching *Roberta* probably didn't realise was that the Paris fashions on display were created by RKO designer Bernard Newman, born in Joplin, Missouri, who came direct from the Bergdorf Goodman department store, New York, where he was Head Designer. When Texan Travis Banton first came to Paramount, the studio publicity department claimed their new designer was from Paris. MGM managed to entice Adrian back into films for *Lovely To Look At* (1952), the Technicolor remake of *Roberta*. He had left MGM in 1942 to open a private dressmaking salon in Beverly Hills and insisted the costumes be made in his own workrooms and not the studio's. However, Kathryn Grayson, who plays the manageress of a Parisian dress salon, was not too happy with the frilly dresses she had to wear. The contrast between the fashion parades of

the two films, seventeen years apart, reveals much about the difference between 30s and 50s styles, and shows how time alters the concept of glamour. For *Roberta*, Newman had flowing silks and gold and silver lamé gowns, while Adrian's were closer to Dior's New Look. Christian Dior himself only worked a few times for the cinema, his one musical being *Gentlemen Marry Brunettes* (1955), a feeble farrago which finds Jeanne Crain and Jane Russell in Paris and on the Riviera.

The American fashion photographer Richard Avedon was the 'visual consultant' on *Funny Face* (1957) and French designer Hubert de Givenchy created Audrey Hepburn's Paris wardrobe. (Edith Head did the rest.) It was Givenchy's first film and he

ABOVE *Jane Powell, the winsome, nubile soprano singing 'It's A Most Unusual Day' from* A Date With Judy *(1948), the usual bright, family fare offered by MGM, wholesome as distinct from sensual, glamour.*

BELOW *MGM's young thrush, Jane Powell in* Three Daring Daughters *(1948), accompanied by 'long-haired' Spanish pianist Jose Iturbi, sugaring the classical pill for audiences of fluffy musicals.*

ABOVE *RKO art directors'
conception of a chic Parisian
dress salon in* Roberta *(1935)
where the fashion parade finale
takes place of the collection
designed by Bernard Newman,
to the apt accompaniment of
Jerome Kern's 'Lovely To
Look At'.*

Seine. Astaire sings the title song in the ruby red glow of a photographer's dark room. Most of the film's exteriors were shot in Paris by director Stanley Donen and cinematographer Ray June, counterbalancing the artificiality of the subject. On first arriving in Paris, Astaire, Thompson and Hepburn go their different ways seeing the sights and singing 'Bonjour Paris', but all three end up at the same time on top of that monument to *chic* – The Eiffel Tower. A montage shows Hepburn being photographed in different outfits in different parts of the city, each shot frozen in negative, then black and white and finally colour. In one of them, she runs down the steps below 'The Winged Victory' in the Louvre, clad in scarlet and imitating the posture of that famous mutilated statue.

In general, film-makers seldom needed to venture beyond the borders of Los Angeles in order to make Paris into Paree. MGM built Paris in America for *An American in Paris* (1951) which included the eighteen-minute ballet in which celebrated landmarks are depicted in the styles of Dufy (Place de la Concorde), Renoir (Pont Neuf), Utrillo (Montmartre), Rousseau (the zoo at Vincennes), Van Gogh (Place de L'Opera) and Lautrec (the Moulin Rouge). Film director George Cukor and his art director Gene Allen, visited Paris to make sketches and gather material for *Les Girls* (1957) but, said Cukor, 'I think we managed to capture the essence of Paris without using any genuine Parisian shots. Although later against my better judgement, I let them put in a couple of long shots of

was to become Hepburn's favourite designer, making five more films with her. Fred Astaire plays Dick Avery (Richard Avedon?) a photographer, and Kay Thompson, a magazine editor based on Carmel Snow of *Harper's Bazaar*. It tells of intellectual Audrey Hepburn being discovered in a book shop in Greenwich Village and her transformation into a top fashion model. Although the content of the film is simple-minded, the form is sophisticated. Colour is the dominant feature, from the opening number, 'Think Pink', to Hepburn in a bridal gown surrounded by white swans and doves on the apple-green banks of the

RIGHT *Kay Thompson (centre),
editor of a New York fashion
magazine, advising her staff to
'Think Pink' in Stanley Donen's*
Funny Face *(Paramount 1956),
another musical where the world
of* haute couture *provides the
glamorous background.*

the real city.' Most of *Gigi* (1958) was actually shot in Paris, the principal sites being the Bois de Bolougne, Maxim's and the Tuileries gardens. The location shooting during a hot summer caused many of the women extras, in heavy *fin-de-siecle* fashions and tight corsets, to faint. The eminent photographer and designer Cecil Beaton, making his first Hollywood film, is credited with the costumes, production design and scenery. Against the art nouveau decor of Maxim's, move violet, lemon and emerald dresses of satin, velvet and silk, encrusted with layers of jewels and set off with bird of paradise plumage. The final scene is an animated Renoir painting of the Bois de Bolougne with its ladies on horseback, military officers, children playing with their nursemaids, women of the world parading with boulevardiers. Among all this splendour Leslie Caron, having 'grown up in the most delightful way', appears in an open carriage, wearing a brocaded lilac lace dress, with a bonnet of ostrich feathers and branches of egret. All

this prompted Stanley Kauffmann in *The New Republic* to write, 'The real star is Cecil Beaton. When the story ambles and the songs don't quite soar, the clothes and settings continue to enchant. A deaf man could enjoy *Gigi*.'

Although the lewdness of the original French novella by Colette has been sugared over, the story of two old cocottes raising a young girl to be a courtesan recalls the land of the 30s Paramount musical, especially with the captivating presence of Maurice Chevalier. As he sings 'I'm Glad I'm Not Young Anymore' and 'Thank Heaven For Little Girls', his enduring charm dispels any unpleasantness from the subject. The voice evokes the flavour of the Lubitsch operettas in which he romanced Jeanette MacDonald in a gilded palace of some distant country. 'Ah, yes, I remember it well!' he sighs. Set in a sumptuous Paris and starring Chevalier, Ernst Lubitsch's *The Love Parade* (1929) was one of the first musicals written especially for the screen. *Gigi* was among the very last.

❛*If all the French finery impresses the customers, it also smothers the story . . . the physical exuberance of the production flusters the pensive sensuality of Colette's mood.*❜

Time Magazine on Gigi (1958)

BELOW *The sumptuous Bois de Boulogne climax to Vincente Minnelli's* Gigi *(MGM 1958), with Leslie Caron on Louis Jourdan's arm in Cecil Beaton's stylish period costumes, and assorted* fin-de-siecle *Parisian promenaders in the background.*

ABOVE *Ginger Rogers (2nd left), Ruby Keeler (centre) and Una Merkel (wearing trousers).*   RIGHT *Pert Ann Sothern a sassy blonde.*

GLORIFYING THE AMERICAN GIRL

Beautiful girl, You're a lovely picture,
Beautiful girl, You're a gorgeous mixture
Of all that lies, Under the big blue skies.

Beautiful girl, You're a dazzling eyeful,
Beautiful girl, I could never cry
For if I had you, You'd be a dream come true.

Lyrics by Arthur Freed
from *Going Hollywood* (1933)

*T*he early screen musical was not only the domain of sophisti-cated Europeans satisfying their nostalgia for their homelands by creating golden dreams; it was also peopled by newly-arrived New Yorkers, flashy Broadway impresarios and producers who brought the hurly-burly of The Great White Way into the palm-lined avenues of Hollywood. Not for them medieval chateaux where aristocrats sang duets in heavily draped boudoirs, nor the cafe society of the Champs Elysees. 'Naughty, bawdy, gaudy, sporty' 42nd Street was their favourite thoroughfare. The monarchs of this kingdom were kings and queens of burlesque accompanied by an entourage of high-stepping peroxide chorus girls called Peggy Sawyer, Polly Parker or 'Anytime' Annie. Their cultural heritage was not opera or operetta but vaudeville and the Ziegfeld Follies. The melodies they responded to were not waltzes but 'the hip hooray and ballyhoo. The Lullaby of Broadway.' It was brash, vibrant, gutsy, jazzy. It was American.

The Ziegfeld Follies were created by the most famous impresario of his day, Florenz Ziegfeld. They were a series of illustrious revues that typified Broadway glamour between 1907 and 1931, always featuring a bevy of beautiful showgirls in gorgeous costumes descending vast staircases. The slogan of the Follies was 'Glorifying The American Girl'. Young cuties, who once dreamed of becoming Ziegfeld girls, flocked to Hollywood in the 30s to try their luck in the movies. A copy of *Photoplay* magazine at the time tempted them with 'Remember how many young women have stepped from the pulchritudinous precincts of the

RIGHT *Anita Page (left) and Bessie Love (right) on either side of Charles King in* The Broadway Melody *(MGM 1929), the first musical to receive an Academy Award. The modest feminine chorus line of twelve would soon multiply ten-fold in future movies.*

BELOW *Joan Blondell (left) and Lana Turner (right) putting aspiring musical hopefuls through their paces in* Two Girls On Broadway *(MGM 1940), a revamped version of* The Broadway Melody *(MGM 1929).*

Follies to achieve glory on the screen?' The chorus gave these hopefuls a special group identity. They provided voluptuous backgrounds to the decorously clad stars. The Ziegfeld Follies were the inspiration behind many an early film musical.

The Broadway Melody (1929) was the first all-talking, all-singing, all-dancing movie. It was also the first sound film to be awarded an Oscar for Best Picture and the first MGM picture to get the award. Furthermore, it invented a formula – the 'backstage'

musical – which was to dominate the genre, on and off, for decades to come. The auditions, the rehearsals, the backstage bickering, the wise-cracking chorus girls, the out-of-town tryouts, the financial difficulties, and the final, spectacular, triumphant onstage production, often featuring a youngster taking over the lead at the last moment and achieving instant stardom. Unlike the operetta tradition, people only sang and danced within the confines of a show. The tenuous plot of *The Broadway Melody* tells of the romantic entanglements of the partners of a sister act (Anita Page and Bessie Love) during the run of the latest Francis Zanfield (sic) extravaganza.

Another formula of 1929 was to dispense with plot altogether in favour of a string of statically filmed numbers, occasionally going for a few daring overhead shots of girls in a flower pattern. The first of these was *Hollywood Revue of 1929*, in which a little song by Arthur Freed and Nacio Herb Brown called 'Singin' In The Rain' was first heard. It was introduced by Cliff 'Ukelele Ike' Edwards and chorus dressed in raincoats during a downpour. The two-tone colour finale has Albertina Rasch's dancers in green tutus against a green orchard dotted with oranges. As the sun comes up, so does the entire cast, including Joan Crawford, Marion Davies and Buster Keaton, in transparent raincoats to reprise 'Singin' In The Rain.' 'I don't think I spent more than an hour and a half writing the lyrics,' Arthur Freed recollected many

years later when he was the great producer of MGM musicals. Each studio followed with their own revue in which every star under contract was put on display. Warner Bros'. *The Show Of Shows* (1929) replied to Freed's song with 'Singin' In The Bathtub' performed by Winnie Lightner, former vaudeville singer. This strange hotch-potch also included Bea Lillie, Rin-Tin-Tin, John Barrymore (speaking a Shakespearean soliloquy), Myrna Loy as an oriental princess, and Ann Sothern and Loretta Young among the chorus. Ernst Lubitsch directed three Maurice Chevalier numbers in *Paramount On Parade* (1930) with a grand two-tone Technicolor finale, 'Sitting On Top Of A Rainbow And Sweeping The Clouds Away' in which Chevalier, as a chimney sweep, is surrounded by girls dressed in the various colours of the rainbow. *King Of Jazz* (1930) was Universal's contribution. Directed by John Murray Anderson, his original concepts of staging were to be a marked influence on later numbers.

But no matter what the form, the content remained emphatically feminine. A forerunner of later girlie numbers was 'Turn On The Heat' from *Sunny Side Up* (1929) which opens with a covey of lovelies in Eskimo apparel. As the Arctic locale begins to change to a tropical one, they shed their furs for brief tops and

bottoms. When the heat intensifies, everything catches fire and the girls dive into a surrounding ornamental pool as a sheet of water rises in place of a curtain. Cecil B. DeMille, the maker of opulent peep-shows and pious epics, got into the act with *Madam Satan* (1930), his only musical. It featured a wild costume party sequence (clothes by Adrian) held on a Zeppelin. Each guest enters with a verse explaining his or her costume. One lady, clad only in a few strategically placed fans, is 'Miss Movie Fan' while

ABOVE *The grand finale of* Hollywood Revue Of 1929 *(MGM) with Buster Keaton (2nd left), Marion Davies, Joan Crawford, and Cliff 'Ukulele Ike' Edwards with chorus, reprising Arthur Freed-Nacio Herb Brown's 'Singin' In The Rain'.*

LEFT *Warner Bros.' answer to MGM's 'Singin' In The Rain' number from* Hollywood Revue Of 1929, *was 'Singin' In The Bathtub' in* The Show Of Shows *(1929) performed by the portly vaudeville artist Winnie Lightner.*

'*Out of 100 odd girls on the lot, they took an average and found the ideal chorine to have 32½" bust, a 23" waist, hips 34", calf 12½", ankle 7½". Venus de Milo, with her 28½" waistline, couldn't get a job as script girl on Poverty Row.*'

Article in Photoplay 1929

Henry VIII appears with his six wives dressed in shining cellophane. Finally, the eponymous villainess materialises in a black velvet cloak with a squined serpent's head on the back. A floor show includes an electric ballet with some dancers dressed as spark plugs. Florenz Ziegfeld himself surpervised *Glorifying The American Girl* (1930) at Paramount, which served as a showcase for torch singer Helen Morgan, leaning against a white grand piano and warbling 'What Wouldn't I Do For That Man', Eddie Cantor, Rudy Vallee and, naturally, a parade of smiling girls doing the Ziegfeld-trained walk.

MGM paid three extravagant tributes to Ziegfeld, starting with *The Great Ziegfeld* (1936), made four years after his death. The cantankerous, consumptive, womanising Ziegfeld was played by suave William Powell in this romanticised show-business biopic. It showed Ziegfeld launching his Follies in 1907, followed his marital and financial problems, and ended with his death at 65, still dreaming of mounting another show. Mostly undistinguished, the film is remembered mainly for the mammoth 'Pretty Girl Is Like A Melody' number (staged by Dave Gould) which ends the first half of this three-hour movie.

ABOVE RIGHT *A high camp musical sequence from Florenz Ziegfeld's* Glorifying The American Girl *(Paramount 1930), glorifying the American Boy as well, in 'The Garden Of Love' finale. It was the only film the great impresario 'supervised' himself.*
RIGHT *Virtuoso dancer Ray Bolger doing the splits in front of a vast dishful of delicious Ziegfeld beauties in the 'She's A Follies Girl' number from* The Great Ziegfeld *(MGM 1936).*

LEFT *The pinnacle of MGM extravagance: the 'Pretty Girl Is Like A Melody' production number from* The Great Ziegfeld *(1936), with its multitude of cat-costumed showgirls and a male chorus, in top hats and tails, singing to the accompaniment of numerous Wurlitzers with more girls in white gowns arranged on revolving Doric columns.*
BELOW RIGHT *A grandiose column built to the glory of each drum-major chorus girl, with five panting collie dogs, in a number from* The Great Ziegfeld *(MGM 1936).*
BELOW LEFT *William Powell (centre with jacket off) as* The Great Ziegfeld *(MGM 1936), here down on his luck in contrast to the glorious days of his glamorous Follies when he was king.*

Added after regular shooting was completed, and costing a record $220,000, it featured a gigantic revolving spiral wedding cake structure. On a stairway stands Dennis Morgan (dubbed by Allan Jones) in top hat and tails singing the Follies theme song while 192 singers and dancers interpolate extracts from the popular classics. The camera works its way up towards Virginia Bruce, the Spirit of the Follies, perched on top of the edifice, against a starry sky, as billowing satin curtains descend in folds around it. *Ziegfeld Girl* (1941) focused on the lives of three contrasting Ziegfeld showgirls; Judy Garland becomes a star, Lana Turner doesn't, and Hedy Lamarr settles for a domestic life. Lamarr just looks vacantly beautiful wearing frocks by Adrian at his most self-parodic. As she remarked, 'Any girl can be glamorous, all you have to do is stand still and look stupid.' In the tropical production number, 'Minnie From Trinidad', she carries huge orchids on her bust, right hip and head, while Judy Garland's dress pushes her waistline down almost nine inches. Due to clever editing, the film ends with Garland on top of the same wedding-cake set that once held Virginia Bruce in *The Great Ziegfeld*. (There is an amusing spoof of a Ziegfeld show in *Funny Girl*, 1968, when Barbra Streisand disrupts a typically lavish number by entering as a manifestly pregnant bride.)

The closest equivalent to a Ziegfeld show in the cinema was *Ziegfeld Follies* (1946). It returned to the revue format of earlier years and was introduced by William Powell as Ziegfeld, looking down from a blue heaven. After a puppet prologue of the stars of the past, Ziegfeld introduces his show with the possibility of using the great stars of the present. 'How would I

ABOVE *Bedecked in flamboyant creations by Adrian (from left to right), Lana Turner, Judy Garland and Hedy Lamarr pose in* Ziegfeld Girl *(MGM 1941).*
RIGHT *The shapely nymph of the musical – the Prima Ballerina of the Water – Esther Williams, executing a sub-aquaballet in* Ziegfeld Follies *(MGM 1946).*
OPPOSITE *In the same movie, luxuriantly plumed and pink-gowned Lucille Ball bringing an erotic allure to 'Bring On The Beautiful Girls'.*
BELOW *Another still from the movie showing Louis Bunin's Puppets re-enacting the audiences of yesteryear arriving at the Jardin de Paris.*

open?... Let's see. Well, maybe a beautiful pink number with a beautiful pink and white blue-eyed girl.' Fred Astaire sings 'Bring On The Beautiful Girls' and they appear in pink, on a merry-go-round, seated on live horses. Lucille Ball, bedecked in plumes and a swirling pink cloak, cracks a whip at girls in black-cat costumes and fish-net stockings as they execute a feline dance. The routine ends with unblinking Virginia O'Brien pleading, 'Bring On The Wonderful Men.' The feast continues with contributions from Astaire, Esther Williams, Judy Garland, Lena Horne, Kathryn Grayson and Gene Kelly. Ziegfeld's last words were reputedly, 'Curtain! Fast music! Lights! Ready for the last finale! Great! The show looks good!' He would have been happy that his Follies had continued many years after his death.

Florenz Ziegfeld was one among millions who suffered in the Wall Street Crash of 1929. In that year, he sold the screen rights of his hit stage production 'Whoopee', starring the saucer-eyed singing comic Eddie Cantor, to Samuel Goldwyn. The agreement called for the show to close and Ziegfeld to receive credit as co-producer of the movie. However, Ziegfeld had alienated Goldwyn by insisting on his own name preceding Goldwyn's on the credits so, in the event, Sam barred Flo from the set. The cast of *Whoopee!* (1930) was virtually the same as that of the stage version, but Samuel Goldwyn decided to bring Broadway dance director Busby Berkeley to Hollywood to stage the numbers, and thus revolutionised the concept of glamour in the musical.

Busby Berkeley believed that the film musical was 'terribly static and restricted', but Goldwyn promised him complete artistic freedom. Taking advantage of this promise, Berkeley immediately eliminated three

RIGHT *Saucer-eyed comedian Eddie Cantor in drag (left) with a Goldwyn Girl in Samuel Goldwyn's* Palmy Days *(1931), a frolic set in a health resort overrun by bathing beauties. The ambiguity and exaggeration of drag is used to parody feminine peculiarities.*
BELOW *The Goldwyn Girls providing decorative surroundings for Eddie Cantor as a phony matador in Samuel Goldwyn's* The Kid From Spain *(1932). Betty Grable (4th right) was one of the stars to rise from the ranks of The Goldwyn Girls. Cantor's voracious pursuer, Lyda Roberti, is peeking over his cape.*

of the four camera crews and concentrated on one mobile camera. Many of the earliest musicals were photographed with a stationary head-on camera placed at a long distance from the stage, often reducing the dancers to specks. The camera set-ups varied little from three basic positions, close-up, medium long shot and long shot. Paul Fejos, the Hungarian director, devised a camera crane capable of moving at every angle and a speed of 600 feet a minute for *Broadway* (1929) to impart greater fluidity to the routines. Although in his early musicals, Berkeley borrowed the conventions of the stage, he began to experiment with ways of freeing the musical from its stagey confines.

In the opening number of *Whoopee!* the Goldwyn Girls, dressed in Red-Indian headgear, followed a 14-year-old Betty Grable in a dance, forming an abstract pattern for Berkeley's first overhead shot in the movies. He also decided to film each girl in close-up, a practice he continued throughout his career, thus humanising the abstract, Art-Deco mosaics. 'We've got these beautiful girls, why not let the public see them?' he asked. The Goldwyn Girls were the cinema's answer to the Ziegfeld Girls. They usually acted as decorative backing for Goldwyn comics Eddie Cantor and Danny Kaye. In *Up In Arms* (1944), starring Kaye, the setting of an army ship imprisons their shapely figures in khaki uniforms until an ornate dream sequence allows them to wear flimsy negligées. Busby Berkeley used the Goldwyn Girls in the four Eddie Cantor musicals he made. To illustrate the song 'Bend Down, Sister' in *Palmy Days* (1931), Berkeley's camera moved along the cleavage of each Goldwyn Girl as she bent down. *The Kid From Spain* (1932) opened in what was supposed to be a girls' dormitory. There, the Goldwyn Girls as college students (!), rose from their sumptuous satin beds in transparent nightdresses. The setting of the 'No More Love' number in Berkeley's final film for Goldwyn, *Roman Scandals* (1933), was a slave market in which nude girls wearing long, blond wigs almost down to their knees, were chained to various pedestals. 'I asked the girls if they would mind being photographed nude provided it was done in a beautiful and artistic manner by dressing their hair over their breasts etc', Berkeley remembered. 'They said they would do it if I would close the set and film it only at night to avoid unnecessary visitors.' There was also the tantalising suggestion of nudity (and a striking use of revolving mirrored doors) in a Roman bath-house where Cantor, as a eunuch in blackface, urges about 100 girls to 'Stay Young And Beautiful'. The odalisques were half-dressed by John Harkrider, the designer of many Ziegfeld shows. In the Goldwyn musicals in which an array of sparsely-dressed, beautiful, ever-smiling

BELOW *The incomparable dance director Busby Berkeley (left) on the set of* Roman Scandals *(Goldwyn 1933), with Eddie Cantor in black face. Berkeley got his start in the movies with the Cantor vehicles in which he manipulated the Golwyn Girls into sensuous patterns.*

females draped themselves around pillars and clutched pillows, Berkeley extended the role of the chorus, bringing eroticism to the fore. However, it was not until he was able to make use of the superior technical expertise available at Warner Bros. that he began to create his most memorable work.

The Warner musicals, born of the Depression, were economical, fast-paced and down-to-earth, with a feeling for the social milieu from which they sprang. They contrasted the tales of hard-working chorus girls living in cheap apartments with the lavish production numbers of the shows in which they appeared. Thus the bewitching power of a Broadway show to convert the sordid into the glamorous. There is no clearer distinction between The American Dream and American reality than in the Busby Berkeley-Warner musicals of the 30s. The production numbers seem to have no connection with the rest of the film and could be removed without damaging its structure, but they represent the culmination of the blood, sweat and tears of the rehearsals we have witnessed and an escape from the bitter realities of the Depression. They serve as an opiate, as 'trips' to another world. They reflect our unconscious desires

and awaken the vestiges of our primitive belief in magic. Berkeley's flights of fantasy do not take place within the restricted frame of the proscenium arch, but in the minds of the audience and the celluloid lovers who sing the melody. Berkeley was able to create musical numbers purely in terms of his single choreographed camera, dollying in erotically on the lines of identically-dressed dream girls and forming kaleidoscopic effects with high overhead shots from a mobile crane. Sometimes in order to get high enough, he had to bore holes in the roofs of Warner's sound stages. He also originated monorails to move the camera rapidly over long distances. The camera has a sexual thrust, it is the eye of a *voyeur*. Berkeley's libertinage does not have the subtlety of a Lubitsch, but he transmutes the conventional calendar-girl material into cheerful and lyrical sensuality.

But Busby Berkeley did not work alone. The numbers were the result of close collaboration and integration between a number of people, almost always the same team: camera (Sol Polito), decor (Anton Grot), costumes (Orry-Kelly), musical arrangements (Leo Forbstein), songwriting (Harry Warren and Al Dubin) and production (Darryl F. Zanuck). The non-musical parts of the films were directed by expert Warner contract directors: Lloyd

ABOVE *A montage of the 'Remember My Forgotten Man' number from* Gold Diggers Of 1933 *(W.B.) with its creator Busby Berkeley in the centre, one of the few routines to use a social theme for its background within the glamorous context of the musical.*

RIGHT *Juvenile leads, demure Ruby Keeler and boyish Dick Powell in* Gold Diggers of 1933 *(W.B.), innocents caught in the lewd goings on of 'Pettin' In The Park, one of Busby Berkeley's 'Dirty Joke' numbers.*

Bacon, Ray Enright, Archie Mayo, Mervyn LeRoy and Berkeley himself. The formula plots usually followed the trials and tribulations involved in putting on a Broadway show, ending with the successful opening night. The seedy show business milieu and fancy nightclubs were peopled with tough gold-digging cookies such as Una Merkel, Glenda Farrell and Joan Blondell, sugar daddies Guy Kibbee and Hugh Herbert; slave-driving directors Warner Baxter or James Cagney; and, as innocents in a corrupt world, the juvenile leads Dick Powell and Ruby Keeler.

Boyish, energetic, wavy-haired Dick Powell seemed wide-eyed at finding himself in show business among so many gorgeous chorus girls. He had a dangerously high tenor voice and could hoof a little. In *Footlight Parade* (1933), Powell is brought in and introduced to the dance director, played by Berkeley himself, who takes one look at Powell and says, 'I can't use him.' Ruby Keeler was Miss Ordinary of 1933 (she was also Mrs Al Jolson of 1928–1941) whose voice was a mere squawk and whose round-shouldered tap dancing could be most flatteringly described as The 39 Steps, but as she was the only

featured female solo dancer, her deficiencies were less evident than they might have been. Her dialogue usually consisted of the line, 'Gee, Jimmy/Brad/Billy, that's swell!' As Dick Powell let his libidinous imagination run away with him (in the form of a Berkeley production number), she would stare naively into his eyes. However, his mind is definitely on her when the song 'I Only Have Eyes For You' in *Dames* (1934) is taken to the letter. Everywhere Powell looks he sees dark-haired Ruby. Multitudes of girls have her face, until they all come together to form one huge jigsaw puzzle picture of her simpering visage.

The characteristic Berkeley routine begins with lovers introducing a song in a simple setting, after which the camera sweeps away into a surrealistic world before returning to the duo. They can be divided into 3 categories: Sex Objects, Dirty Jokes and Racy Yarns. A classic example of the first is 'The Shadow Waltz' from *Gold Diggers Of 1933* in which 100 girls, dressed in blonde wigs and white lampshade skirts, play 100 illuminated violins on a series of platforms and ramps. When the lights go out, only the violins can be seen, glowing in the dark and moving to take the shape of one gigantic violin. In *Gold Diggers Of 1935* Dick Powell, dressed in 19th-century costume, sings 'The Words Are In My Heart' to Gloria Stuart before they shrink into porcelain figures in a floral arrangement as 56 girls in white gowns appear, seated at 56 white baby grands. The pianos sweep and swirl in patterns before coming together to form a

AL JOLSON—The Lure of Ruby

'You ain't heard nuthin' yet', Al Jolson rendered at the top of his voice. And truly, we hadn't. He could turn a lullaby as raucous as a subway and, what with *The Jazz Singer* and a previous history as the peak star of an infant recording industry, he was a success.

Yet, as though aware that at any moment the star's nightmare – of a suckered audience demanding back all the loot – might come true, he had a paranoid fear of rivals. If another singer could be heard over the intercom in his theatre dressing room he would pull the plug; his was to be the only voice that should break the silence.

A cantor's son, who became an entertainer in blackface, he had singled himself out, as it were, by way of two ethnic minorities – all the better to seem apart from the rest of us. Disguise is always a formidable source of energy and his energy was revved up ferociously behind all his masks.

His early musicals are dedicated to the principle that nothing succeeds like success – *The Singing Fool, Sonny Boy, Mammy*. Only once did he manage to submerge himself within what approximated to a team-effort with *Hallelujah, I'm A Bum* for director Lewis Milestone.

Jolson's voice was not really meant for movies. It aimed to hit the ears of the vaudeville Saturday-nighter sitting at the back of the topmost gallery. Sound recordists were said to reduce the decibels so as not to go deaf making one of his musicals.

When Jolson, at the age of 46, went courting with Ruby Keeler, who was later to grace so many Busby Berkeley musicals, he had *The Jazz*

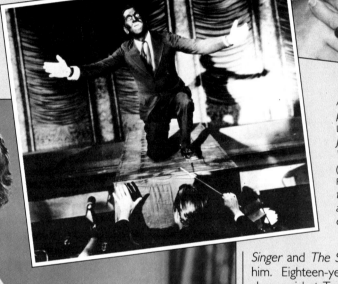

ABOVE *A smiling, confident Jolson photographed in the mid-1930s.* LEFT *The legendary blackface of Jolson, emoting 'Mammy' from Warner Bros.* The Jazz Singer *(1927), the first feature talkie.* FAR LEFT *Ruby Keeler, the not-too-talented 'girl next door', but the apple of Al's eye. They were divorced in 1939.*

Singer and *The Singing Fool* lucratively behind him. Eighteen-year-old Ruby was a simple chorus girl at Texas Guinan's famous nightclub where Jolson was a visitor. Jolson fell in dangerous love. Dangerous, because demure, dimpled Ruby had been friendly for some time with an Italian gangster and bootlegger, known for some peculiarly ethnic reason as Johnny Irish.

The message was out: 'Stay away from Ruby. Or else ...!' To Johnny Irish, Ruby was a pearl beyond price. Besides, Jolson was too old for her. But Jolson persisted in his attentions; he wanted marriage. So Johnny Irish phoned Jolson to say he was coming to have a showdown with him at the Sherry-Netherland hotel in New York where the entertainer was staying. Jolson waited, saying afterwards that the butterflies in his belly had assumed the size of vultures. Irish appeared, asked for a drink and sat down. 'Look pal,' he said, 'If I ever hear from Ruby that you treated her bad in marriage, I'll come and kill you personally.' It was, in its way a kind of blessing. Before he went he turned to Jolson and said 'Good luck!'

ABOVE *Busby Berkeley's staging of 'The Shadow Waltz' in Gold Diggers Of 1933 (W.B.), with girls in identical blonde wigs, swirling their white hooped skirts and playing electrified violins, the first of Berkeley's pageants to feature musical instruments where the girls themselves become instruments.*
RIGHT *The orgasmic ostrich-feather slave galley made up of fifty Busby Berkeley chorus girls in Fashions Of 1934 (W.B.) with a beaming Art-Deco sun as a backdrop, an example of his erotic/exotic dream landscapes in his Garden of Delights.*

dance floor (the pianos were actually lightweight shells carried on the backs of stagehands dressed in black to blend with the black floor). The only production number in *Fashions Of 1934* has 50 girls in ostrich feathers arranged as a slave galleon heaving on a canvas ocean. The girls then metamorphose into the prows of harps being plucked by female harpists swathed in white. Dick Powell falls asleep 'By A Waterfall' in *Footlight Parade* and dreams that Ruby Keeler strips to a swimsuit to join a group of nymphs diving into the water. Photographed from above, they become water-lilies opening and closing, while under water they combine into a vast wheel (predating the Esther Williams aquaballets). 'I designed a special bathing costume with rubber head-pieces looking like hair that ran across the girls' bodies to give a semi-nude effect' explained Berkeley. In the title number from *Dames*, hundreds of chorus girls in white blouses and black tights are seen waking, bathing, dressing, and hurrying to the theatre where they become part of a series of optical mazes. It ends with the girls reclining on different levels of a scaffold structure but, as the camera pulls back, they become tiny figures and, with an imperceptible cut, Dick Powell's head bursts through the picture in close-up.

The 'Dirty Joke' approach is exemplified by the 'Shuffle Off To Buffalo' number from *42nd Street* (1933), which reveals a trainload of honeymoon couples in pyjamas, including newly-weds Ruby Keeler and Clarence Nordstrom. As Keeler prepares for bed, Ginger Rogers and Una Merkel, sharing a berth, comment cynically in song, 'When she knows as much as we know, she'll be on her way to Reno.' The sequel was 'Honeymoon Hotel' from *Footlight Parade*. This time Miss Keeler has just married Dick Powell. He goes to the washroom in pyjamas, but returns to the wrong room. Seeing him with another woman, Ruby threatens to call a lawyer, but believes his story in the end and they go off to bed together. The final shot shows a magazine with a picture of a baby. Most salacious of all is 'Pettin' In The Park' from *Gold Diggers of 1933*, featuring various couples on park benches, as well as a monkey couple in a cage. The scene changes to winter, and enormous snowballs make up all kinds of prismatic patterns. Couples begin petting again when spring returns, until a sudden rain storm drives the girls into a two-level dressing room where they take off their wet clothes in silhouette. A fiendish dwarf-baby (Billy Barty) lifts the shades and they are revealed wearing metal underwear. Dick

'I never had the intention of making eroticism or pornography. I love beautiful girls and I love to gather and show many beautiful girls with regular features and well-made bodies. It is the idea of spectacle which is expressed in 'What do you go for?' What do you come to do, why do you go to a spectacle? It is not the story, it is not the stars, nor the music. What people want to see are beautiful girls.'

Busby Berkeley in 1966

LEFT *Busby Berkeley's water sprites cavorting 'By A Waterfall' in* Footlight Parade *(W.B. 1933), supposedly happening on stage as a 'prologue' to a film, but germinating in the lascivious mind of the dreamer Dick Powell.*

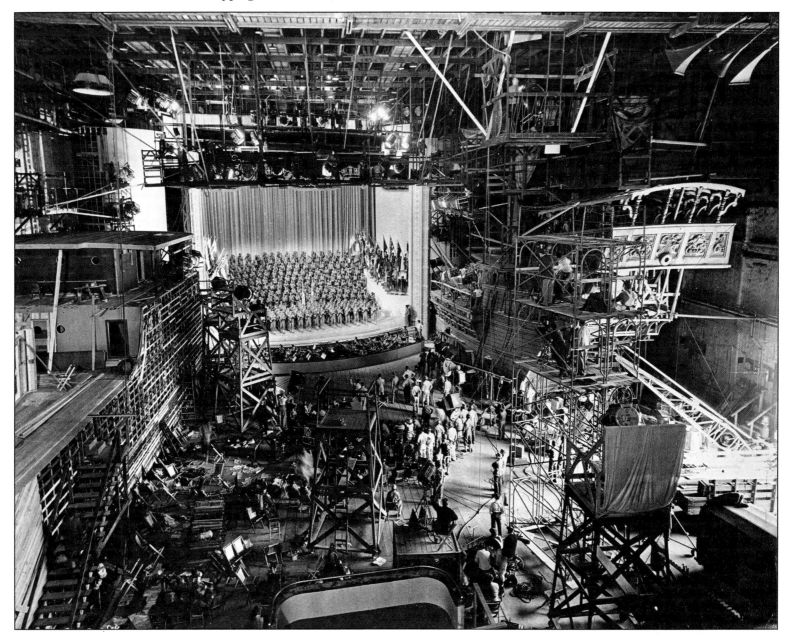

ABOVE *The gigantic sound stage used for* This Is The Army *(W.B. 1943). Irving Berlin's grandiose musical tribute to the armed forces featured 350 actual fighting men as well as a plethora of stars, proving that glamour also resided in the sight of uniforms* en masse.

Powell finds it impossible to cuddle Ruby in that outfit until the little brat hands him a can-opener so he is able to pry open her chastity suit.

Berkeley's sense of the 'Racy Yarn' flavours every moment of the title number from *42nd Street*, as well as 'Lullaby Of Broadway' from *Gold Diggers Of 1935*. The first opens with Ruby Keeler, literally a taxi-dancer, tapping on top of a Checker Cab. Two lovers fight in a hotel room and the girl jumps out of the window into the waiting arms of a boy below. Their dance ends when the jealous lover stabs the girl. Finally, girls carrying large skyscraper cut-outs compose the Manhattan skyline. 'Lullaby Of Broadway' also tells a sordid tale. It opens with the face of singer Wini Shaw as a tiny speck in the darkness which moves nearer and nearer until it fills the entire screen. Suddenly her face turns upside down, the contours making up a section of the Manhattan skyline in a

trompe l'oeil effect. Later she is seen out dancing in a palatial nightclub where 100 dancers in black leather gyrate on several levels to different rhythms, shot from a variety of angles including beneath their tapping feet. Wini rushes to a balcony pursued by the rather menacing, gesticulating crowd. She falls over the ledge to her death and we see the reverse of the opening images. The skyline becomes the face which recedes into the darkness once more. Another musical narrative rhythmically tells the tale of sailor James Cagney searching through the bars and opium dens for Shanghai Lil (a miscast Ruby Keeler) in *Footlight Parade*. They meet in a dive and, after tap-dancing on the bar top, he leaves her to rejoin his ship, but she dons a sailor suit and goes along with him. The sailors go through a routine of complicated military drills, eventually holding up huge cards that make up the Stars and Stripes which change to an image of

President Roosevelt. This finale demonstrates yet another aspect of Berkeley's creative imagination. His military school training had given him a knowledge and passion for army drills reflected in dance routines such as 'All's Fair In Love And War' from *Gold Diggers Of 1937* in which Dick Powell and Joan Blondell (Powell's second wife) lead a company of 70 white-helmeted girls, carrying flags and drums, goose-stepping over a shiny black surface (Mel Brooks in his 'Springtime For Hitler' number in *The Producers*, 1968, parodies Berkeley with an overhead shot of jackbooted chorus girls in the form of a swastika.) Newsreels in the 30s made movie audiences aware of the trappings of fascism and, from today's viewpoint, many of Berkeley's rigorously regimented routines echo the 1934 Nuremberg Rally as witnessed in Leni Riefenstahl's *The Triumph Of The Will*.

Screenwriter Donald Ogden Stewart commented, 'Economically, the Depression had little effect on the people in Hollywood, most of whom never even got near knowing how to spell it. Some of us scriptwriters were disgusted when we watched the producers of lavish musicals spend more and more money on sets and things for films that completely avoided the reality of what was happening in the rest of the country at the time.' The only musical directly about the Depression was the quaint and soft-centred *Hallejulah I'm A Bum* (1933) with Al Jolson as a tramp (happy to be poor) living in Central Park. *Gold Diggers Of 1933*, directed by Mervyn LeRoy, did not avoid the grim reality of the times either. From its ironically optimistic opening, 'We're In The Money' sung by Ginger Rogers and

ABOVE *A high overhead shot from a mobile crane of the bathing beauties in 'By A Waterfall' from* Footlight Parade *(W.B. 1933), one of the many prismatic patterns created by Busby Berkeley before swooping down for close ups of the ever-smiling girls.*

LEFT *Because of budget restrictions, Busby Berkeley staged the number 'All's Fair In Love And War' from* Gold Diggers Of 1937 *(W.B.) effectively without sets, merely using military-style drills as the basis for a symbolic battle of the sexes, against a black background and a shiny black floor.*

t's all too wonderful, and so I'll stick to words

ABOVE *Always going on the assumption that 'big is beautiful', Ruby Keeler and Lee Dixon dance over the giant typewriter keys in the 'Too Marvelous For Words' number from* Ready, Willing And Able *(W.B. 1937), choreographed by Bobby Connolly, attempting to emulate Busby Berkeley.*
RIGHT *Hollywood's influence on Indian musicals is shown in this throwback number from James Ivory's* Bombay Talkie *(1970). Only in musicals are Indians able to circumvent the film restrictions on sex by manifesting it in lavish song and dance routines.*

chorines dressed only in carefully placed gold coins, containing the lines 'You never see a headline, 'bout a breadline today' to the film's ending with one of the rare social conscience numbers in all musicals. Joan Blondell (dubbed by an unknown singer) as a streetwalker, sings 'Remember My Forgotten Man' which tells of the war heroes who are now on the dole. A policeman tries to arrest a hobo for loitering, but Blondell shows him the man's medal. A flashback reveals hundreds of men fighting in the trenches and marching, marching, marching. It then returns to the Depression where the same men are lining up at a soup kitchen. Soldiers marching in silhouette on three levels of a huge archway as Blondell exhorts a crowd of men and women to help them, was an extremely brave way to end a movie in the 30s.

Hollywood Hotel (1938) and *Gold Diggers In Paris* (1938) marked the end of Busby Berkeley's association with Warner Bros. The budgets for musicals were being drastically cut by the studio and public taste was changing. Gone were the opulent sets, complicated overhead shots and the multitude of extras. *Hollywood Hotel* contained a superb sequence set at a drive-in diner using the cars and customers, plus the cinema capital's anthem 'Hooray For Hollywood', sung in a motorcade on the way to the airport to bid farewell to

> *I never cared whether a girl knew her right foot from her left so long as she was beautiful. I'd get her to move or dance, or do something. All my girls were beautiful and some of them could dance a little, some of them couldn't.'*
>
> **Busby Berkeley**

LEFT *Dave Gould choreographed this number from* Folies Bergere *(20th Century-Fox 1935), using Maurice Chevalier's celebrated boater as a mammoth motif with a chorus of Lilliputian dancers dressed in the manner of the French star, a final Hollywood homage before he returned to Europe.*
BELOW *Cy Caldwell on* Gold Diggers Of 1933 *in* New Outlook.

Hollywood-bound Dick Powell. Busby Berkeley was MGM-bound.

Busby Berkeley was such an imposing figure as dance director in the 30s that his influence was felt by many other choreographers who emulated, but never surpassed, him. Bobby Connolly was second string dance director to Berkeley at Warner Bros. from 1934 to 1938. There was more actual dancing in his numbers, but his attempts at Berkeleyesque routines pale by comparison. As *Flirtation Walk* (1934) was dedicated to West Point Academy, the numbers featuring cadets and their girl-friends, led by the inseparable Dick Powell and Ruby Keeler, are devoid of prurience. Al Jolson and Ruby Keeler in *Go Into Your Dance* (1935) – the only film they made together – sing 'Latin From Manhattan' in a nightclub which opens up into a Spanish setting and ends, for some reason, with the two of them on top of an enormous globe. The closest Connolly came to Berkeley was in *Ready, Willing And Able* (1937) with its gigantic typewriter on which 32 girls' legs encased in black tights form a typewriter-ribbon, while Ruby Keeler and Lee Dixon dance over the keys spelling out the lyrics of 'Too Marvelous For Words.' Connolly moved over to MGM in 1939, at the same time as Berkeley, where he did his best work on *The Wizard Of Oz* (1939) and *Broadway Melody Of 1940*.

At Paramount, Mitchell Leisen's *Murder At The Vanities* (1934) rivalled Berkeley in eroticism if not in artistry. It included riotous routines in which semi-nude girls cuddle on giant powder puffs, Kitty Carlisle swims through a sea of undulating plumes waved by chorines, Gertrude Michael sings 'Sweet Marijuana' against a background of phallic cacti, and 'Cocktails For Two' celebrates the end of Prohibition. Other Berkeley-influenced numbers sprang up all over the place. In Fred Astaire's first film, *Dancing Lady* (1933), Sammy Lee and Eddie Prinz created 'That's The Rhythm Of The Day' using the activities of a crowded street containing the transformation of elderly women into glamour girls by a beauty-salon. Dave Gould was responsible for the spectacular aerial ballet finale of *Flying Down To Rio* (1933), which featured about a dozen chorus girls in revealing costumes with hair streaming, dancing on the wings of a fleet of aeroplanes above Rio. One of the girls falls, but is caught on the wings of a plane swooping below. Gould also provided the numbers for *Folies Bergere* (1935), one of which uses leading man Maurice Chevalier's famous straw hat as a motif, including one big enough for a chorus to dance around; and another with several dozen girls making half-hearted patterns with umbrellas in 'Rhythm Of The Rain' (a sequence at the Folies Bergere, with topless girls was made for the French version.)

The nostalgia industry has produced many attempts at Busby Berkeley homage and parody. Ken Russell's *The Boy Friend* (1971) inflated Sandy Wilson's modest 20s pastiche into an all-ogling, all-winking, all-nudging, all-knowing 30s musical, missing the point of

THIS laugh-filled, heart-warming musical comedy romance would be thoroughly delightful from beginning to end if the producers had thrown away the last reel, which unwinds the woes and tribulations of 'My Forgotten Man' who went to war and then to seed, causing untold anguish to the lady who sang of his troubles, while we were treated to flash-backs of marching soldiers, wounded soldiers and discharged soldiers... A veteran myself, I can take most war films cheerfully on the chin, but I want none of them in musical comedies, where they certainly do not belong. For downright offensiveness and bad taste, that last reel wins the Croix de Garbage.

RIGHT *Ken Russell's inflated pastiche of Busby Berkeley's Warner Bros. musicals in* The Boy Friend *(MGM-EMI 1971), with flapper girls whirling around on a gramophone record to produce a rather strained kaleidoscopic effect, another nostalgic trip to the musical's glorious past.*

BELOW *From his cinema seat, the depressed hero (Steve Martin) of* Pennies From Heaven *(1982), literally projects himself into* Follow The Fleet *(RKO 1936), taking Fred Astaire's place and dancing with his mistress (Bernadette Peters) as Ginger Rogers, a demonstration of the musical's ability to transform a drab life into a glamorous one.*

Berkeley's numbers by stressing their 'period charm'. The famous shot from 'Young And Healthy' in *42nd Street* where the camera moves through a tunnel of female legs ending with a close-up of a leering Dick Powell and Toby Wing, is slavishly copied. The best spoof of a 30s Warner Bros. musical is 'Baxter's Beauties Of 1933', the second half of Stanley Donen's double bill *Movie Movie* (1978). The dialogue of mixed metaphors and crushed clichés is delivered straight-faced by the cast including a bouncing Dick-Powell-like singer-composer and a dizzy, innocent Ruby Keeler type. Michael Kidd, the choreographer, never attempts to equal the Berkeley style except for one token overhead shot. The use of colour is unauthentic and so is the camp extravagance of the star's dressing room. *Pennies From Heaven* (1982), the most telling view of glamour in the 30s, expresses how escapist musicals were perceived during the Depression. The down-beat contrast between the fantasy on screen and the reality is forcefully portrayed in the title number, sung by a tramp as gold coins drift down from the sky against pictures of destitute people. Songs are depicted as anti-Depression drugs and dreary surroundings are changed into dazzling settings by words and music. 'There must be some place where the songs come true', says the hero (Steve Martin) who literally gets lost in a Fred Astaire film. Coming out of the theatre into the rain, he says 'It's always the same. You come out of the movies and the goddam world has changed.'

At MGM, Busby Berkeley had to adapt to the sexless house style and generally bring out the best in the youthful duo of Judy Garland and Mickey Rooney. At Warners, no-one cared if he cut away from Dick Powell and Ruby Keeler to concentrate on the female figments of his male chauvinist imagination, but the

ABOVE *Busby Berkeley moved from the adult girlie fantasies at Warner Bros. to the adolescent freshness and vitality of Judy Garland and Mickey Rooney at MGM, seen here in 'Hoe Down', an enthusiastic, flowing musical number from* Babes On Broadway *(1941).*

LEFT *The expansive and dazzling Busby Berkeley minstrel number, with Mickey Rooney in the chair, from* Babes On Broadway *(MGM 1941), a favourite tradition of pre-Black rights musicals. Women usually appeared wearing a light tan make-up.*

RIGHT *The versatile Mickey Rooney dragged up as Carmen Miranda in* Babes On Broadway *(MGM 1941), creating camp out of camp while gesturing madly and singing 'Mama Yo Quiero' Senorita Miranda herself coached Mickey in the impersonation.*

raison d'être of the MGM production numbers was to display the buoyant talents of Rooney and Garland. Despite six films with Berkeley, Judy had an aversion towards him. His intense rehearsal schedules did not suit her nervous temperament. 'I used to feel as if he had a big black bullwhip and he was lashing me with it,' she recalled. 'Sometimes I used to think I couldn't live through the day.' However, Berkeley's inventive contribution to these 'barnyard musicals' was inestimable. His intricate camera set-ups and the vitality and enterprise of his choreography gave a lift to the 'gee-kids-let's-put-on-a-show' format. *Babes In Arms* (1939) climaxes with a patriotic pageant 'God's Country', containing nearly 100 healthy-looking dancers and musicians (no lines of platinum blondes) who claim, 'We've got no Duce, no Fuhrer, we've got Garbo and Norma Shearer.' Another of Berkeley's military routines closes *Strike Up The Band* (1940) showing how superb editing can substitute for lavish sets, and the spacious minstrel show finale of *Babes On Broadway* (1941), raises the distasteful 'happy nigger' formula into a zestful entertainment. The latter includes a hilariously accurate impersonation of Carmen Miranda, 'The Brazilian Bombshell', by

RIGHT *Busby Berkeley's fantastical phallic number, his first in glorious Technicolor, from* The Gang's All Here *(20th Century-Fox 1943), a logical aesthetic conclusion to his sex and symbol conceptions – girls manipulating giant bananas in 'The Lady With The Tutti-Frutti Hat'.*

'*As it turned out we realised there was no shot of Mickey and Judy making up in blackface, so the audience didn't know it was Mickey and Judy. It was a good lesson; if you are ever going to show someone in disguise, you better show them putting it on. So we did a retake showing Mickey and Judy getting into blackface . . . then the number went like a house on fire.*'

Roger Edens, associate producer of
Babes On Broadway *(1941)*

LEFT *The flamboyant, exotic 'Brazilian Bombshell' Carmen Miranda of the extravagant gestures, bizarre costumes and fruity headgear, a caricature of South American womanhood, contrasted with the American girl in a string of 40s Fox musicals.*

Mickey Rooney complete with make-up, fruity headgear, bare midriff and extravagant gestures.

The real Carmen Miranda appeared in Berkeley's first film in Technicolor, *The Gang's All Here* (1943) at Twentieth Century-Fox. Away from the sanitary restrictions and teenage troupers at MGM, he was given the money and freedom to indulge his Freudian fantasies once more. 'The Lady With The Tutti-Frutti Hat', a bizarre sequence, is set on a banana plantation. Sixty female pickers lounge about until Carmen Miranda enters singing the self-descriptive song while the girls do suggestive things with 60 giant bananas. The final shot is of Miranda in front of a backdrop of hundreds of bananas that look as though they are part of her already fantastical headdress as huge strawber-

ries grow on either side of her. (This high-camp phallic number was cut from the film in some S. American countries.) The finale involves two 50-foot high revolving mirrors which create endless patterns for the dancers placed between them, and the disembodied heads of the leads float about on a field of amber and gold as they each sing a line from the song, 'Journey To A Star'. It was Yvonne Wood's first film as costume designer, most of her ideas going to Carmen Miranda's head.

Back at MGM, Berkeley paid tribute to Ann Miller's legs in 'I've Got To Hear That Beat' from *Small Town Girl* (1953) by having 50 musicians in holes in the dance floor with only their intruments and hands visible, playing upwards to the vigorously tapping

BELOW *Only the lusciously leggy Ann Miller is seen in 'I've Got To Hear That Beat' from* Small Town Girl *(MGM 1953), Busby Berkeley's choreographic and musical instrument tribute to her dynamic tap dancing.*

Miller. Busby Berkeley made his final splash in the stunning aquaballets he created for Esther Williams, the prima ballerina of the water. In *Million Dollar Mermaid* (1952), 400 streams of water shoot up 30 feet from a vast tank, forming a gigantic waterfall. Miss Williams emerges on top of a geyser and dives into the pool. In an overhead shot that recalls the best days at Warner Bros., 100 swimmers do aquabatics in circular patterns as Williams rises like Aphrodite from the sea surrounded by nymphs with 500 multicoloured sparklers and yellow smoke as a background. The water skiing ballet in *Easy To Love* (1953) was filmed on location at Cypress Pleasure Gardens in Florida. Over 30 water skiers are towed in arrow-head formation with Esther Williams at the tip. They jump

and slalom around the lovely amphibian in Cinema-Scope and Technicolor. Then, seizing a trapeze dangled from a helicopter, she rises and rises to a height of 500 feet and dives into the lagoon.

Busby Berkeley, born William Berkeley Enos in 1895, died in 1976. He was rediscovered by a new generation in the kitsch cult of the late 60s, and his reputation has grown ever since. He has survived taunts of vulgarity, sexism and automatonism to become the prime motion-picture painter of exotic/erotic dream landscapes framed euphemistically in the tinsel and glitter of the Hollywood musical. Berkeley's glorification of the American girl in his own Garden of Delights is also a panegyric to the magical medium of cinema.

BELOW *The beauteous Aqua-Queen Esther Williams rising triumphantly from a pool, against a background of multi-coloured smoke in Busby Berkeley's climactic water pageant in* Million Dollar Mermaid *(MGM 1952), evoking memories of the myriad of nymphs in 'By A Waterfall' in* Footlight Parade *(W.B. 1933).*

ABOVE *Fred Astaire in his celebrated top hat, white tie and tails.* RIGHT *Astaire with fellow trouper Judy Garland.*

THE LIGHT FANTASTIC

Dance embodies and exalts the spirit of the film musical. The impulse to dance supplies it with an athletic *joie de vivre*, rhythmic ingenuity and kinetic charm. The camera allows the performer to transcend the limitations of a theatre stage, and heightens the sense of continuity in space. The musical, the ultimate fantasy movie, shows the human body in full flight, satisfying the voracious visual demands of cinema. Dance on film had to break with stage conventions to be reconstructed in terms of photography, lighting, sound and editing. It was placed inside the magic box and reappeared as a different art form. The best screen dances are those that combine cinematic invention with actual physical grace. Dance, at its best, is poetry in motion.

However, the marriage of dance and film has not always been an easy one. Lovers of dance as a theatrical medium missed the dancer's corporeal presence and shuddered at the thought of an ersatz dancer on the screen. Their fears were justified in the early days of sound when the cumbersome and stationary camera made dance routines seem flat and lifeless. Sometimes the dancers were reduced to specks while the many concealed microphones made the sound of dancing feet drown out the music. The static adaptations of Broadway shows favoured singers rather than dancers. There had been more fluent demonstrations of dancing in the silent era. The most popular ballroom dancers of the day, Vernon and Irene Castle, appeared in a loosely biographical film, *The Whirl Of Life* (1914), showing all aspects of their art. Joan Crawford made her

RIGHT *Ballet was an important ingredient in the musical, and French* danseuse *and cabaret star Zizi Jeanmaire, seen here in* Black Tights *(1960), brought sensuality to her* pas de-deux *on screen.*

name in pre-sound 'musicals' as the original flapper in *Our Dancing Daughters* (1928) and *Our Blushing Brides* (1928), lively expressions of the Roaring 20s.

Born Lucille LeSueur, she was rebaptised Joan Crawford by MGM who ran a magazine contest to find her a new name. She sang and danced 'I've Got A Feeling For You' and 'Singin' In The Rain' in *Hollywood Revue Of 1929*, and the musical gained its first glamorous dancing star. After a mere four musicals, she became 'the shopgirls' delight' in soap operas, only to return to the genre fourteen years later for *Torch Song* (1953), her first film in colour. Looking stylish in costumes designed by Helen Rose, she played a tough Broadway star who is softened by blind pianist Michael Wilding. Forty-nine-year-old Crawford, as svelte as ever, moves through a horrendous production number called 'Two-Faced Woman', staged to a playback originally filmed for *The Band Wagon* (1953). Twenty years earlier in *Dancing Lady* (1933), she played a chorus girl who makes it to Broadway stardom on her own merits, refusing rich playboy Franchot Tone, and marrying impecunious

RIGHT *Although much of their footwork was 'doubled' by other dancers, Carole Lombard and George Raft were convincing enough in* Bolero *(Paramount 1934), dancing a tango devised by LeRoy Prinz to the pulsating rhythms of the Ravel piece in a Moorish-style nightclub.*

dance director Clark Gable (with whom she made eight pictures; Gable, the epitome of male glamour, was not, in fact, a musical star). Conventional clothes did not suit Miss Crawford's figure, with its wide shoulders, long waist and short legs, so MGM designer Adrian came up with the idea of making her shoulders even broader, enveloping them in ruffles or shoulder pads. 'Who could ever believe my whole career would rest on Joan Crawford's shoulders,' Adrian later remarked. The rest of her appearance was also overstated. Enormous eyes and a large mouth widened with 'The Crawford Smear.' In one number in *Dancing Lady*, 'Heigh Ho, The Gang's All Here', she is partnered by a lean-faced, agile young man in top hat and tails making his first screen appearance. His name was Fred Astaire.

Fred Astaire is the supreme dancer, male or female, in the history of the cinema. He remains unsurpassed in invention, virtuosity and elegance. The top hat, white tie and tails with black cane conjure up Astaire as much as oversize shoes, baggy trousers, battered bowler hat and elastic walking-stick evoke Chaplin,

'*If I'm copied, it's because of my clothes, and Adrian does those. Adrian taught me so much about drama. Everything must be simple, simple, simple. He made me conscious of the importance of simplicity.*'

Joan Crawford

ABOVE LEFT *Fred Astaire making his screen debut in* Dancing Lady *(MGM 1933), with the first of his many female dancing partners, the glamorous Joan Crawford with the gash-smile, in a number called 'Heigh Ho, The Gang's All Here', already wearing his characteristic top hat and tails.*

LEFT *The irresistible Clark Gable facing Joan Crawford on the set of* Dancing Lady *(MGM 1933), a perfect match of the king and queen of Hollywood, an explosive combination that produced eight pictures.*

RIGHT *Astaire displayed his extraordinary dexterity by dancing up and down the walls and on the ceilings of his London hotel room because of the love of Sarah Churchill in Stanley Donen's first film as solo director,* Royal Wedding *(MGM 1951).*

BELOW *'The Carioca', the dance extravaganza that brought the screen's most celebrated dance team together for the first time in* Flying Down To Rio *(RKO 1933). Fred Astaire and Ginger Rogers are seen as the focus of the fantastic Brazilian fiesta on top of seven white grand pianos.*

his antithesis. Astaire is the personification of finesse. A flawless figure floating across the screen. He is the terpsichorean muse of the musical, the patron saint of hoofers. 'The nearest we are ever likely to get to a human Mickey Mouse,' wrote Graham Greene of the way he often moved like a cartoon character, drawn by a fine pencil the tip of which is just off screen. Astaire even walked sweetly. His light, carefree, expressive singing voice inspired the best songwriters. He had a relaxed, boyish, frivolous personality and would chuckle, sing or dance away any sadness that crept into his elfin eyes.

Born Frederick Austerlitz in 1899, Fred Astaire began his dancing career at the age of seven in a vaudeville act with his sister Adele. They became Broadway's top dancing team, appearing in ten musical comedies together. When Adele retired into marriage in 1932, Fred entered films. A studio talent scout commented notoriously on his first screen test, 'Can't act. Can't sing. Slightly bald, Can dance a little,' but David O. Selznick at MGM thought he had

charisma 'in spite of his enormous ears and bad chin line', and gave him a guest spot in *Dancing Lady*. Fred Astaire's attitude differed from Busby Berkeley's way at Warners. 'Either the camera will dance or I will, but both of us at the same time. That won't work,' Astaire said, but he understood the relationship between the cinema and dance. He made every graceful gesture immediately legible to the camera. Although he himself did not direct and seldom took screen credit for the choreography, his creative genius informs all his films. He was a perfectionist who concerned himself with all aspects of filming the dances. He experimented with the possibilities of extending the range of dancing by using slow motion, multiple images, animation, trick photography, but never hindered the purity of his dancing, either solo or in empathy with his many dancing partners.

LEFT *Fred and Dolores del Rio dancing head to head in* Flying Down To Rio *(RKO 1933).*

The setting is an outdoor nightspot in *Flying Down To Rio* (1933). A group of Brazilian singers is performing 'The Carioca', a samba in which some of the steps require the partners to press their foreheads together. On the sidelines are Fred Astaire and Ginger Rogers who become intrigued by the rhythm of the dance. Suddenly, they take to the dance floor for the first time together. They soon have the floor to themselves, watched by admiring couples. The admiration for the pair extended far beyond those on screen to millions throughout the world. Fred and Ginger had two-stepped into the dance hall of fame.

Twenty-two-year old Ginger Rogers, a cheeky, blonde, had already made nineteen films to Fred's one. His classy coolness and her brash ardour complemented each other perfectly, making him warmer and her more remote. Each of their lithesome duets were mini-dramas containing all the attraction, antagonism, and romance of a relationship between a man and a woman, symbolic representations of love-making. Fred woos her with delicate handpasses, she rejects him by swirling away, he draws her to him, she succumbs, the dance works up into a climax and ends on a gentle, satisfied note. The seductive harmony of movement is counterpoised by the monochromatic meeting of her glittering whiteness and the sombre sheen of his black tails. This was given its expression in nine black-and-white RKO musicals between 1933 and 1939, light-hearted comedies of errors whose naive plots and dialogue clashed with the sophisticated cosmopolitan settings. Van Nest Polglase and Carroll Clark were responsible for the polished Art Deco sets of stylised, fashionable resorts, luxurious hotels, palatial ocean liners, and ornate chrome-plated nightclubs with black, glass floors over which the couple glided. Pandro S. Berman produced seven

of the movies, Mark Sandrich directed five. Original songs were written by Irving Berlin, Jerome Kern, Cole Porter and George Gershwin, the enduring giants of songwriting. The supporting cast usually included unctious Eric Blore, prissy Franklin Pangborn and fussy Edward Everett Horton. Choreographer Hermes Pan assisted Astaire on the dance routines and also dubbed in the sound of the taps. Bernard Newman set the standards for the couple's fashion-plate elegance with his costumes.

If the plots were very much alike, so was the musical programme. There were generally two duets, one of a flirtatious, competitive nature, and the other a lilting, passionate one. Astaire's two solos are contrasted in a similar manner. The first occurs spontaneously in mundane surroundings – in a hotel room, a shop or in the street – with Fred informally dressed, while the second takes place on stage in evening clothes. The production numbers, in four cases, introduce a fabricated new dance, such as the aforementioned 'Carioca'. The 'dangerous rhythm' of 'The Continental', 'a way of dancing that's strictly *entre nous*', was presented in *The Gay Divorcee* (1934), the film version of the Broadway hit 'The Gay Divorce', but the Hays Office claimed that a divorce should never be gay. Today, there would be more objection to the adjective rather than the noun. 'The Continental' is a 17-minute routine in which Fred and Ginger lead dozens of dancers through a tango and Russian dance variations. 'The Piccolino' in *Top Hat* (1935) is performed during a carnival in a dazzling, white Venice in which the incomparable couple give an extraordinary exhibition of ballroom dancing to the

BELOW *Fred Astaire and Ginger Rogers would always discard their formal attire and perform more relaxed and breezy duets, often baiting each other capriciously. The RKO costume designers gave Ginger an equal variety of gorgeous ballroom gowns and sporty wear.*

Haystack' (*The Gay Divorcee*). As he puts on his tie and jacket, handed to him by his valet, he begins irresistibly to dance at the same time. After leaping over sofas and chairs, he catches his hat, twirls his umbrella and exits. Again in a hotel suite in *Top Hat*, he taps furiously around, waking up Ginger in the room below, as Edward Everett Horton watches with a mixture of admiration and dismay. In the title number, Astaire dons his talismanic top hat, white tie and tails in 'an atmosphere that simply reeks of class' and executes a series of breathtaking arabesques and entrechats. After making tauromachian moves with his cane, he uses it as a rifle to mow down a chorus of similarly attired male dancers, his taps simulating the sound of shots. Fred's fleet feet provide the close-order drill for a navy of tapping sailors in 'I'd Rather Lead A Band' from *Follow The Fleet* (1936), and 'Slap That Bass' in *Shall We Dance* (1937) finds him dancing in the spotless engine room of an ocean liner, his taps synchronised with the pounding pistons. In *Swing Time* (1936), Astaire pays tribute to the great black dancer Bill 'Bojangles' Robinson with 'Bojangles In Harlem'. (Jerome Kern only managed to compose it after Fred had spent an afternoon tapping around Kern's hotel suite). Astaire, in black face, does a Bojangles-like solo in front of three enormous shadows of his dancing self projected on the wall behind him. His devastating dexterity is demonstrated in *Carefree*, where he manages to hit eight golfballs in a row

ABOVE Follow The Fleet (*RKO 1936*) cast the debonair Astaire as a gum-chewing sailor, which didn't prevent him from donning his customary white tie and tails at the finale. The cup he is holding with Ginger Rogers was won in a dance contest in the movie.

astonishment of local revellers. *Carefree* (1938) offered 'The Yam' in which Fred and Ginger get the members of a swanky country club to join in as they wind exhilaratingly in and out of rooms and across terraces.

Astaire's solos are the purest examples of *élan* in dance that the cinema has to offer. In his hotel room, he takes off his dressing gown and sings 'Needle In A

RIGHT A ballet dream sequence, artily choreographed by Roland Petit, in Daddy Long Legs (1955), takes place in the mind of waif Leslie Caron, imagining how her rich patron (Fred Astaire) looks. The lurid De Luxe Color was characteristic of 20th Century-Fox films of the period.

straight down the fairway, dancing and singing at the same time to impress Ginger. All to no avail, as she had left just before he started the routine.

Great as the solos and production numbers are, there is nothing more memorable in the nine movies than the grace and line of movement, the chemistry and collusive interaction between Fred and Ginger in their duos. Their screen partnership reflected a close and amicable relationship that could withstand the gruelling rehearsals, and the camera acted like the Fairy King's love juice, transforming them into lovers on screen. After the romantic duet 'Night And Day' (*The Gay Divorcee*), Ginger sinks into an armchair, gazing up at Fred in wonderment. Fred seduces her while dancing 'Cheek To Cheek' (*Top Hat*) but, at the end, she slaps his face. 'She loves me!' he exclaims. He fails to win her over in 'Never Gonna Dance' (*Swing Time*), which takes place in a deserted nightclub. They hold each other closely, but she achingly spins away from him and the dance ends in separation. Sometimes they bait each other capriciously as in 'Isn't It A Lovely Day' (*Top Hat*). Taking shelter from the rain in the bandstand of a London park, they challenge each other with tap steps until thunder drives her into his arms. They bicker breezily in 'Let's Call The Whole Thing Off' (*Shall We Dance*) in Central Park where they perform a flowing dance on roller-skates which becomes a frenzied chase, ending with them falling laughing on the grass. 'A Fine Romance' (*Swing Time*),

shows the temporary cooling of affection, each accusing the other of being 'as cold as yesterday's mashed potatoes.'

The duets are not only gems studding the stories but, far more than the dialogue, trace the emotional development of the two characters and even advance the plot. In order to get to meet dancing teacher Rogers in *Swing Time*, Astaire pretends he can't dance a step during a lesson. Blaming Ginger for Fred's two left feet, her boss Eric Blore fires her. Fred gets her her job back by demonstrating the skills she has taught him in just one lesson. The title number from *Shall We Dance*, proves that Fred is in love with Ginger when he appears with girls all wearing Ginger Rogers masks.

While Fred's costume remained reassuringly unchanging, Ginger Rogers was supplied with a selection of seductive gowns that also enabled her to move gracefully. Bernard Newman designed a wet-look seal gown and black satin slippers for her in *Roberta* (1935). She wore a chiffon dress covered with crystal beads in *Follow The Fleet*, which clung tight to her body but blossomed out when she danced. At times, the lighting would give her dresses a transparency that revealed her legs. In exchange for the screen rights of *The Story Of Vernon And Irene Castle* (1939), RKO agreed that Irene Castle should design Ginger's dresses. Ginger refused to have her long hair

I HAD been watching Ginger and Fred rehearsing. Tirelessly, almost religiously – over and over and over, perfecting perfection. And watching Ginger, in pale yellow overalls, pale green polo shirt, red-gold hair flying...I thought, she has everything...yes, in spite of what may have grieved her and caused her separation from Lew (Ayres, 2nd husband). She has youth and beauty and fine feathers. And she has Fred Astaire for a dancing partner. 'Yes, I get what I want from life except time. Time to go to college, time to be a house-wife, time to have a baby, time to be normal.'

ABOVE *Gladys Hall writing in Photoplay 1939.*
LEFT *Fred Astaire in* Roberta *(RKO 1935), greeting Ginger Rogers who is passing herself off, complete with a thick Polish accent, as Countess Tanka Scharwenka and wearing a silver fox fur cape and hat, one of the first of Bernard Newman's many creations for Ginger on the screen.*

RIGHT *The wondrous duet to Cole Porter's 'Begin The Beguine' from* Broadway Melody Of 1940 *(MGM), performed with breathtaking aplomb by Fred Astaire and the stylish Eleanor Powell, the only film in which they danced together.*

cut in a bob, and had secret meetings with designer Walter Plunkett who made subtle changes in the dresses. Both leads felt restricted in their roles, which was not helped by the domineering and fastidious presence of Irene Castle on the set. The final film in the remarkable RKO sequence, it was also their least successful. The public found it hard to accept the idea of Astaire dying in a film (Castle was killed in a plane crash), even though the movie ends with his ghost dancing a last waltz with his widow. The film was a pale echo of their earlier triumphs, and Fred and Ginger decided to go their separate ways.

The sole picture Astaire made away from Rogers in the 30s was *A Damsel In Distress* (1937). When both Ruby Keeler and English star Jessie Matthews were unavailable, RKO settled for the non-dancing Joan Fontaine. There is an unconsummated duet which cries out for Ginger Rogers. However, Astaire is involved in seven scintillating Gershwin numbers including 'Nice Work If You Can Get It' in which he performs a dynamic drum solo and dance. It also gives his comic talent full play, flanked as he is by comedians George Burns and Gracie Allen, especially in a joyous fairground scene, spectacularly designed by Van Nest

ABOVE *Fred with the winsome but musically miscast Joan Fontaine, in* Damsel In Distress *(RKO 1937), set in a castle in England where Fred dances frustratingly around the non-dancing Fontaine.*
RIGHT *Fred Astaire had no more ravishing partner than flame-haired Rita Hayworth, seen here in the aptly titled* You Were Never Lovelier *(Columbia 1942), dancing with him to Jerome Kern's 'I'm Old-Fashioned'.*

Polglase with distorting mirrors and revolving floors and walls. As Fred did not have a female dancing partner, comparisons with Ginger were avoided. But in *Broadway Melody Of 1940*, Fred joined MGM's top dancing star, Eleanor Powell, who was essentially a soloist. Brilliant as they were together, they somehow remained separate entities who failed to cohere as Astaire and Rogers could. The highlight of the film is the 'Begin The Beguine' finale staged by Bobby Connolly. Dressed in fanciful Latin-American clothes, Powell and Astaire trip along a glittering black-mirrored floor over their own reflections against a starry background.

Paulette Goddard (nearing the end of her marriage to Chaplin) was an uninspiring partner in *Second Chorus* (1940), before Astaire's relatively successful two-film collaboration with Columbia Pictures' classiest star, 23-year-old Rita Hayworth. Known as Rita Cansino until 1937, she began her dancing career in her father's Spanish dancing act. Turned redhead and anglicised, this sensuous, statuesque beauty was dissimilar to Ginger Rogers, who happened to be her cousin by marriage. Her dances with Fred enlivened the creaky plots of *You'll Never Get Rich* (1941) and *You Were Never Lovelier* (1942). In the latter, they perform a dance around the spacious gardens of a South American villa, going from classical steps to modern via Latin American, to the tune of Jerome Kern's 'I'm Old-Fashioned' – an epithet, alas, equally applicable to the film.

Meanwhile, at MGM, under producer Arthur Freed's tutelage, musicals were moving towards a more integrated form where character, dialogue, plot, decor and music fused into a whole. From the peak of 30s black-and-white musicals, through the valley of the early 40s, Fred Astaire managed the leap into the Technicolored, surreal world of MGM's visual tone poems. Although the image of the top-hatted, white-tied dandy from an earlier era still clung to him, he made the transition with exceptional ease in *Yolanda And The Thief* (1945) and *Ziegfeld Follies* (1946). His partner in both was the strangely expressionless, red-haired dancer Lucille Bremer. However, by now the partnerships were becoming secondary to the all-absorbing *mise en scene* of these 'dance stories'. As the sad-faced Chinese coolie in love with a harlot in the 13-minute 'Limehouse Blues' segment from *Ziegfeld Follies*, Astaire brought a tragic dimension to his dancing. He dies in a London street after dreaming a love duet in an Oriental setting.

The past was evoked in the 'Puttin' On The Ritz' number from Paramount's *Blue Skies* (1946) in which Fred is backed by a row of miniature multiple images

of tapping top-hatted Astaires. Mark Sandrich, who had directed six of Astaire's films, died of a heart attack at the age of 45 during shooting. The picture, contrary to its title, was dull, and Astaire declared *Blue Skies* to be his last film. However, after two years of retirement, he was called back to MGM for *Easter Parade* (1948) when Gene Kelly broke his ankle. Because of their different styles, the dance routines were reworked by Astaire. Typical were 'Drum Crazy', performed in a toy shop and demonstrating again his adroitness with drum sticks, and 'Stepping Out With My Baby', a technical triumph using slow motion and normal motion in the same image. Joining Judy Garland for the clownish duet, 'A Couple Of Swells', Fred plays against his polished persona by impersonating a tramp with a battered top hat and missing front teeth.

Garland and Astaire were to be linked again in *The Barkleys Of Broadway* (1949), but because of Judy's erratic behavior and nervous illness, she was removed

ABOVE *The two greatest male dancing stars of the cinema, Astaire (left) and Gene Kelly, together in George Gershwin's 'The Babbitt And The Bromide' from* Ziegfeld Follies *(MGM 1946), comically using their supposed rivalry in their dance routine. They were reunited 30 years later in* That's Entertainment Part 2 *(MGM 1976).*

'*When we finally got around to shooting our first dance, I thought for some reason Ginger seemed taller than usual. I asked (Hermes) Pan, 'Am I crazy or is Ginger on stilts?' He said 'I know something is different.' I went to Ginger. 'Hey' I said 'have you grown or have I shrunk?' She laughed and confessed she had sneaked some higher heels over on me.'*

Fred Astaire on **The Barkleys Of Broadway** *(1949)*

RIGHT *Fred Astaire and Ginger Rogers in their Technicolor reunion in* The Barkleys Of Broadway *(MGM 1949), attempting to recapture that first rapture in a reprise of George and Ira Gershwin's 'They Can't Take That Away From Me'.*

RIGHT *'The Shoes With Wings On' number from* The Barkleys Of Broadway *(MGM 1949), choreographed by Hermes Pan, in which a shop of shoes dance by themselves. A disembodied but breathtakingly dexterous Astaire supplied all their dancing.*

from the picture. Arthur Freed got the idea of contacting Ginger Rogers for a reunion with Astaire after ten years. 'Gin and I had often discussed the possibility of getting together for a rematch. And here it was, out of a clear sky.' Their pleasure at working together again was somewhat soured by the arrival of Garland on the set during the shooting, wearing one of the costumes for the film and hurling insults at Ginger. She was finally led away by director Charles Walters. Except for the 12-year delayed encore of Gershwin's 'They Can't Take That Away From Me', first sung by Astaire to Rogers in *Shall We Dance*, the duets had Ginger but not much zip.

In the latter years, as important to Fred's sartorial imagery of top hat and tails, were shoes. Shoes that traced the movement of his flashing feet. This is recognised at the start of *Silk Stockings* (1957), when the camera follows only Fred's brown suede shoes and white socks as they leave a hotel room, wait impatiently for an elevator and get into a cab. As they alight, the shoes suddenly leap into a trot and we see their famous owner. It is perfectly natural that in *The Band Wagon* (1953), a downhearted Astaire should be cheered up by a shoeshine in a 42nd Street amusement arcade. With 'A Shine On Your Shoes', he takes off on a tapping tour-de-force around the array of slot-machines. Hermes Pan's 'Shoes With Wings On' number from *The Barkleys Of Broadway* has Fred as a shoemaker whose shoes start to dance by themselves (their tapping was supplied by a disembodied Astaire). He puts a pair on and they cause him to dance sublimely. The other pairs of shoes join in frenziedly until Fred stops them by firing two pistols. After a dance in *Top Hat*, Edward Everett Horton had exclaimed, 'Say, you have wings!' Fred completely disregards the law of gravity in *Royal Wedding* (1951), by dancing on the walls and ceiling of his London hotel room (the effect was achieved by having a camera affixed to the floor which then revolved as Astaire danced). In *The Belle Of New York* (1952), he floats to

ABOVE *Currier and Ives turn-of-the-century prints provided the inspiration for this number from* The Belle Of New York *(MGM 1952), with Vera-Ellen and Fred Astaire in a summer scene, one of the four seasons they dance through together.*

LEFT *Even in a relatively drab dress, Cyd Charisse hots up the Cold War in a number called 'The Red Blues' from* Silk Stockings *(MGM 1957), supposedly performed in an equally drab Moscow, to contrast with the glamour and glitter of Paris.*

ABOVE *Fred Astaire as a Private Eye, and tantalizing gangster's moll Cyd Charisse, revealed as 'Mr Big', in the Mickey Spillane spoof 'Girl Hunt' ballet from Vincente Minnelli's* The Band Wagon *(MGM 1953), choreographed by Michael Kidd.*

the top of Washington Square arch and then dances on passing clouds, after a kiss from Vera-Ellen.

The Band Wagon provided the occasion for Astaire's propitious meeting with the glorious, classically trained, ballerina Cyd Charisse. Long-limbed, dark, erotic Charisse brought out a tougher, sexier side of Fred's dancing. Their first *pas de deux*, 'Dancing In The Dark', in the simple, nocturnal setting of Central Park, recalls the best and more lyrical of the Astaire-Rogers duets. They glide, spin, leap and sway in the blue shadows, rapt in each other, finally relaxing in a horse-drawn carriage. Even as the caricature Soviet commissar in *Silk Stockings*, Charisse, with severe hairstyle and little makeup, admits to 'the urge to merge with the splurge of the Spring,' as Cole Porter's lyrics put it. Astaire sways in front of her

as an invitation to dance. Immediately in his arms, she becomes a sinuous female, using steps obviously learnt at the Russian ballet. In a solo dance in her Paris hotel bedroom, she strips off her heavy, green velvet dress and black woollen stockings and puts on the hose of the film's title, silk and satin underwear, silver high-heel shoes, diamond earrings and a frivolous Paris hat. Clothes have transformed her into the incarnation of 'capitalistic' glamour.

The top hat, white tie and tails of Astaire are seen behind the titles of *The Band Wagon*, the film that self-mockingly portrays him as out of key with the artistic pretensions of the choreographer and director of a Broadway musical. Later, he dons his familiar formal garb, with British star and fellow old-timer Jack Buchanan, in a soft-shoe, 'I Guess I'll Have To Change

LEFT *Leslie Caron (centre) in virginal white in a rosy ballet scene from 20th Century-Fox's CinemaScope production of* Daddy Long legs *(1955). Caron's freshness, Frenchness, gamine looks and delicate dancing were used effectively in a number of 50s musicals set in a fantasy France.*

My Plan' – elegance personified, and in *Silk Stockings*, he tips his top hat in the direction of the current youth craze in 'The Ritz Roll And Rock', much of it danced by the chorus on their stomachs on the floor. As Fred sings in the same film, 'It's not enough to see a dancer at his ease, he's got to put his back out and come sliding on his knees.' Although his dancing belied his age, Astaire's last three dancing partners, Leslie Caron in *Daddy Long Legs* (1955), Audrey Hepburn in *Funny Face* (1957) and Cyd Charisse were 32, 30 and 22 years his junior respectively. After *Silk Stockings* (excepting *Finian's Rainbow*, 1968), Fred entered the less spectacular realms of character acting, retiring from the musical as only Fred Astaire could – gracefully.

'If I'm the Marlon Brando of dancing, Fred Astaire's Cary Grant', conceded Gene Kelly, the other great male dancer in the Pantheon of musicals. Comparisons may be odious, but they are often revealing. Astaire's evening wear contrasted with Kelly's T-shirt and jeans and the most celebrated sailor-suit in films besides Donald Duck's. Astaire was more ethereal, Kelly more corporeal. Astaire had a slightly shy self-deprecating smile, Kelly's broad Colgate grin was part of his aggressive self-confidence. There is a braggadocio approach to his personality and dancing, and he sings 'I Like Myself' in *It's Always Fair Weather* (1955) with conviction. Kelly is perfectly happy alone, Astaire is disconsolate as he sings 'I Go My Way By Myself' in *The Band Wagon*. Astaire strutted, Kelly swaggered. While we remember Astaire's partnerships, it is Kelly's solos that really ignite the screen. Kelly lacked the selflessness to blend with a female

dancing partner. His best duets were with other men, where a sense of rivalry rather than romance suited his personality better. With The Nicholas Brothers in the acrobatic 'Be A Clown' number from *The Pirate* (1948), with Frank Sinatra and Jules Munshin in the exuberant 'New York, New York' from *On The Town* (1949), with Donald O'Connor in the terrific, tongue-twisting tapper, 'Moses Supposes' from *Singin' In The Rain* (1952), and the street dance with Michael Kidd and Dan Dailey with garbage-can lids attached to their feet in *It's Always Fair Weather*. Astaire and Kelly

BELOW *Audrey Hepburn in black sweater, jeans, white socks and pumps, escapes the rigours of being an exquisite fashion model in Paris by performing a frenetic Apache-type dance in a smoky, Left Bank cellar with two Beatniks in Stanley Donen's* Funny Face *(Paramount 1956).*

ABOVE *Gene Kelly, in his distinctive sailor suit, appears with a cartoon figure in the 'Sinbad The Sailor' episode from his own* Invitation To The Dance *(MGM 1956), an ingenious combination of live-action and animation in dance.*

forces in the heyday of the musical in the 50s. His virile, athletic, earthy and inventive dancing combined acrobatics, tap and ballet, and he was perfectly at ease as the swashbuckling D'Artagnan in the non-musical, *The Three Musketeers* (1948). He made his film debut at MGM with Judy Garland in *For Me And My Gal* (1942). It was her first adult role but her fifteenth movie and Kelly remembers her helping him through this melodramatic musical set during World War I. In Garland alone did he find a female counterpart. As the doyenne of American movie critics, Pauline Kael, observed, 'She joined her odd and undervalued cake-walker's prance to his large-spirited hoofing, and he joined his odd, light, high voice to her sweet deep one.'

Kelly's ingenuity had its first chance to emerge in 'The Mop Dance' from the revue-style morale-boosting *Thousands Cheer* (1943). As a soldier made to clean the local PX, he takes up his mop as a dancing partner, then uses it as a gun aimed at a poster of Hitler, his machine-gun tapping providing the sound of shooting. A more attractive partner was the lovely, made-for-Technicolor redhead Rita Hayworth in *Cover Girl* (1944). Many of the numbers fore-shadowed the future Gene Kelly. Singing 'Make Way For Tomorrow', Kelly, Hayworth and Phil Silvers dance joyously down a Brooklyn street, meeting a policeman, tap-dancing with a milkman and helping a drunk. Kelly, alone on a deserted street at night, sees his reflection in a shop-window. It eerily takes on a life of its own and tempts him to give up the girl he loves.

danced together in 'The Babbitt And The Bromide' episode from *Ziegfeld Follies* as two solid citizens who greet each other with the same small talk every time they meet, even when they are harp-playing white-bearded angels. Although the hoofing is superb, it is all rather self-congratulatory. Kelly later remarked, 'I thought I looked like a klotz.' Only thirteen years younger than Astaire, Kelly seems to exist in another time sphere altogether.

Gene Kelly entered movies from Broadway (he was 30) in 1942, when the film musical was going through its crucial transitional stage. As dancer, choreographer and director, he became one of the most creative

RIGHT *Donald O'Connor (left) and Gene Kelly in loud checked suits doing a corny vaudeville number called 'Fit As A Fiddle' in* Singin' In The Rain *(MGM 1952), an ironic comment on Kelly's claim that whatever he did, he had 'dignity, dignity'.*
FAR RIGHT *Fred Astaire (left) and Gene Kelly, the great veteran dancers from the golden age of musicals in* That's Entertainment Part 2 *(MGM 1976), still 'tripping the light fantastic', although not as light or as fantastic as they once were.*
OPPOSITE *The ultimate glamour girl, Rita Hayworth, posing for a magazine pin-up in Charles Vidor's* Cover Girl *(Columbia 1944). The statuesque redhead brought a healthy eroticism to the role of the chorus girl whose face and figure light up the news-stands.*

THE CROONERS

The crooners were the jock saxophones to compare with the androgynous flutes that had gone before. Charles 'Buddy' Rogers was typical. Wavy-haired, he was the college boy hero of such early Paramount effusions as *Close Harmony* (1929) or *Safety In Numbers* (1930) or *Old Man Rhythm* (RKO, 1935). Dick Powell's voice, too, strayed to the falsetto, but the energy of the kind of musicals he was in – *42nd Street* (1933); *Gold Diggers Of 1935* (1935) – transferred their vitality to him. Besides which, the girls in his movies always seemed to be in a certain sexual danger from him.

Movies cannibalised radio for most of its singing men on the principle that if you can't beat 'em, buy 'em in. Rudy Vallee insinuated a little nasal tonality into the sound of movies via *George White's Scandals* (1934) or *Gold Diggers In Paris* (1938).

The transformation, though, towards a richer sound, came with Bing Crosby whose distinctive, lilting style was first heard with Paul Whiteman's band. Crosby's was a voice that could have come from one of the jug bands in his native Tacoma; an analogy made more definite by his slightly jug-ears. With that sound, the girls knew where they were.

What, then, to make of Frank Sinatra, whose perfectly pitched, mellow notes wafted on to the musical sound-tracks on the strident winds of teenage adulation? There is, encapsulated within the history of the Sinatra voice, almost a history of crooning itself – from youthful reediness to mature maleness.

OPPOSITE *Bing Crosby (left) with ace comedian Danny Kaye, who also crooned from time to time in his films. They are seen here in a number from Irving Berlin's* White Christmas *(Paramount 1954).*
TOP *'Old Blue Eyes', Frank Sinatra (left) and 'The Old Groaner', Bing Crosby, in MGM's* High Society *(1956).*
ABOVE *Youthful and relaxed, like his light tremolo voice, Warner Bros.' crooner of the 1930s, Dick Powell.*

LEFT *Charles 'Buddy' Rogers embraces Baron the dog.*
RIGHT *Bandleader and vocalist Rudy Vallee. His biggest-ever song hit was 'I'm Just A Vagabond Lover'.*

The dance is a duel/duet with his alter-ego, a superb example of both physical and cinematic technique serving each other. *Anchors Aweigh* (1945) contained a live-action cartoon sequence in which Kelly in sailor suit teaches Jerry Mouse how to dance. In the same film, he displays his athletic prowess in a Mexican dance. Wearing a gold shirt, red and black cape, and tight black trousers, he scales battlements, leaps parapets and jumps from a rooftop to a balcony.

Dressed up as a combination of Douglas Fairbanks Sr and John Barrymore, Kelly, in dark curly hair and moustachio, relishes his role in *The Pirate* as an itinerant actor taken for the notorious Black Macoco. Through the sleepy, candy-coloured Caribbean town, he springs from one beautiful girl to another greeting her as 'Niña,' which Cole Porter rhymes with neurasthenia, seen ya, gardenia and schizophrenia. He climbs balconies, slides down a pole, takes a cigar from a girl's mouth, inhales, kisses her and blows out

RIGHT *Gene Kelly made all the nice girls love a sailor. In this scene from* Anchors Aweigh *(MGM 1945), he and Frank Sinatra (foreground), the bobby soxers' delight, prepare for a four-day leave in Hollywood.*
BELOW *Kelly in his most swashbuckling and exuberant form in Vincente Minnelli's* The Pirate *(MGM 1948), walking a tightrope to his lady's chamber, cheered on by the occupants of the colourful Caribbean town.*

the smoke. Later, he performs a furious Pirate Ballet against a background of cannon fire and billowing mauve smoke. In contrast, Kelly celebrates his Irishness in 'The Hat My Father Wore On St Patrick's Day' in *Take Me Out To The Ballgame* (1949), jauntily tapping and pirouetting. In *Summer Stock* (1950), he executes a series of airplane spins on a table, egged on by the handclapping of onlookers singing 'Dig, Dig, Dig For Your Dinner.' In the same movie, standing alone on an empty stage, he builds a dance around a creaky floorboard and a rustling outspread newspaper with masterful simplicity. Gene Kelly made dancing seem the most natural activity – an extension of walking – with the street as his favourite stage. As *An American In Paris* (1951), he delights a group of Montmartre street urchins by getting them to shout the first two words of 'I Got Rhythm', while he demonstrates the third as well as imitating an aeroplane, Charlie Chaplin and a cowboy. Escaping into a roller-rink with gangsters on his tail in *It's Always Fair Weather*, he forgets to take his skates off when he goes back into the streets and whirls along the immaculate New York sidewalks singing 'I Like Myself' and even tap-dancing. (The number took twelve days to rehearse and four days to shoot.)

The apotheosis of Gene Kelly – *danseur extraordinaire* – is the liberating title number from *Singin' In The Rain*. In love, Kelly walks out into the 'California dew' under an umbrella. He puts his hand out to feel the rain, shrugs his shoulders and folds his umbrella. As 'the sun's in his heart' he has no need for shelter. He clings onto a lamp-post, his arms outstretched 'laughing at clouds, way up in the sky.' Then he stands under a drainpipe, splashes in the gutter, jumps into puddles and swings round and round holding his

ABOVE *Gene Kelly at the climax of a show in the barnyard musical to end all barnyard musicals,* Summer Stock *(MGM 1950). Kelly could make jeans or a T-shirt appear as the height of masculine chic.*

LEFT *Kelly in his favourite posture, arms outstretched self-confidently, and lapping up the camera in 'The Broadway Ballet' from* Singin' In The Rain *(MGM 1952), which gave him the chance to demonstrate his ability in several styles of dance.*

umbrella at arm's length as the camera lifts in a breathtaking crane shot. A policeman watches him suspiciously, so Kelly hurries away, handing his umbrella to a drenched passerby. 'The real work for this one was done by the technicians who had to pipe two city blocks on the backlot with overhead sprays, and the poor cameraman who had to shoot through all that water. All I had to do was dance.'

Gene Kelly's female dancing partners included the sweetly virginal All-American Vera-Ellen of the elegantly turned up nose and toes; the *jolie-laide* French gamine Leslie Caron, and the voluptuous Cyd Charisse. Vera-Ellen is miscast as a blonde gangster's moll in the vigorous 'Slaughter On Tenth Avenue' ballet in *Words And Music* (1948), but convincing as the elusive 'Miss Turnstiles' in *On The Town*. Leslie Caron was discovered by Kelly in Paris when she was a dancer with the Roland Petit ballet. Her classical training and naive charm served her well in *An American In Paris*, especially in 'Love Is Here To Stay', dancing with Kelly through the morning mists rising from the Seine. But macho Kelly only met his match with Cyd Charisse. She takes away his 'male initiative' in *It's Always Fair Weather*, by being able to

ABOVE *A girl (Vera-Ellen), a boy (Gene Kelly), a ballet bar, a spotlight, rehearsal clothes, and a sailor suit was all that was needed to create magic in this moment from 'The Day In New York Ballet' from* On The Town *(MGM 1949).*

RIGHT *Voluptuous* femme fatale *Cyd Charisse meets hick hoofer Gene Kelly in 'The Broadway Melody' ballet from* Singin' In The Rain *(MGM 1952), the first time Charisse revealed that she was something more than just another pretty, smiling chorus girl.*

recite the names of all the heavyweight boxing champions. She also shows some nifty footwork in a boxing-ring dance while being praised by a chorus of pugilists who sing, 'Baby, You Knock Me Out.' The 'Broadway Rhythm' ballet from *Singin' In The Rain*, gave Kelly his first opportunity to dance with Cyd Charisse. As a bespectacled, hick hoofer, he arrives in the big city intoning 'Gotta Dance, Gotta Dance.' He gets his chance in a speakeasy where he meets *femme fatale* Charisse. In a loose emerald-green 20s dress, Louise Brooks hairdo and sporting a mile-long cigarette-holder, she balances his hat on the end of her foot, her crossed legs extending almost beyond the frame. But it is Gene Kelly who dominates the number and whose fixed smile fills the screen at the end.

F emale dancing stars have usually been treated as adjuncts to the two great male dancers. Two ladies, however, danced on their own two feet – Eleanor Powell and Ann Miller. Eleanor Powell was billed in the 30s as 'The World's Greatest Tap Dancer' and 'The Queen Of Ra-Ta-Taps.' Louis B. Mayer gave her the lead in *Broadway Melody Of 1936*, although she

had only appeared briefly in *George White's Scandals* (1935). To beautify her homely features for the screen, she had her teeth capped, her hair dyed red and her face experimented on for days by the studio cosmeticians to achieve a glamorous effect. Their achievement was moderate, but there was nothing wrong with her below the neck. Her rapid-fire tapping beat a tattoo through three *Broadway Melodies* (1936, 1938, 1940) and, the appropriately named, *Born To Dance* (1936), all backstage stories with Powell getting her big break in the end. In the latter, the scriptwriters didn't seem to care that Virginia Bruce, a singer, is replaced by Powell, a dancer, just before opening night. The finales mainly involved Eleanor in silver top hat and spangled tuxedo dancing on a battleship with sequined cannons and hundreds of singing and dancing sailors. (She retired from the screen in 1943 to become Mrs Glenn Ford.)

Eleanor Powell's successor was rosy-cheeked, raven-haired Ann Miller. She made eighteen low-budget musicals before her MGM debut in *Easter Parade* (1948), cast against Irving Berlin's wishes. But she stops the show with 'Shakin' The Blues Away', a dynamic solo on a bare stage in which she spins like a

' ***The kiss at the end of Singin' In The Rain was my first French kiss. I didn't know what it was, but now I've learned to like them. Oh, I could tell you some stories about Gene Kelly!'***

Debbie Reynolds in 1974

BELOW *George Murphy in Broadway Melody Of 1940 (MGM), had the unenviable task of seeking comparison with Fred Astaire by dancing with Eleanor Powell in the same film, but acquitted himself well in this elegant 'Between You and Me' number.*

LEFT *Delicious dynamo Ann Miller (with fan) dancing up a storm for the benefit of (left to right on settee) Ron Randell (as Cole Porter), Kathryn Grayson, and Howard Keel, in 'Too Darn Hot' from* Kiss Me Kate *(MGM 1953).*

tapping top. In *On The Town* (1949), she plays an anthropologist(!) who throws herself at Jules Munshin whose face she compares to a prehistoric man. 'Oh, sailor. I love you for having that head!' She then goes into a thrilling, gyrating dance around the Museum of Anthropological History which ends with the collapse of a dinosaur skeleton. Her best role came in *Kiss Me Kate* (1953) which gave her four devastating numbers. Dressed in a brief, luminous red costume in 'Too Darn

Hot', she is at her sexiest kicking those famous legs at the camera in this made-in-3D movie.

The male dancing scene was so dominated by Fred Astaire and Gene Kelly, that their shadows were cast over many other very fine dancers. Another Gene, amiable fair-haired Gene Nelson, pranced through fluffy, Technicolor Doris Day and Virginia Mayo Warner Bros. musicals in the 50s. There were also gangling, eccentrics such as Dan Dailey, Ray Bolger and Buddy Ebsen (a female version being flat-footed, high-kicking Charlotte Greenwood), and energetic pint-sized Donald O'Connor, whose electrifying comedy-dance routine, 'Make 'Em Laugh', from *Singin' In The Rain* was the peak of his career. Unique among them was the cocky, multi-talented James Cagney. Alas, there are too few examples of Cagney's elastically alert hoofing on film, but enough to prove that the gangster movie's gain was the musical's loss. He became the first male Oscar winner in a musical for his portrayal of Broadway song-and-dance man George M. Cohan in *Yankee Doodle Dandy* (1942) in which he taps, springs, sings, emotes and with head forward and bottom sticking up, does the Cohan strut. Cagney made a guest appearance as Cohan in *The Seven Little Foys* (1955), hoofing with Bob Hope to

LEFT *Bill 'Bojangles' Robinson
with little Shirley Temple doing
the 'Polly Wolly Doodle' stair
dance routine from* The Littlest
Rebel *(20th Century-Fox 1935),
one of four movies the great
black tap dancer and the curly-
headed moppet made together.*

BELOW *The superb husband-and-
wife dance team of Marge and
Gower Champion embellishing
the Kathryn Grayson-sung
'Smoke Gets In Your Eyes' from*
Lovely To Look At *(MGM 1952),
a Technicolor remake of the Fred
Astaire-Ginger Rogers musical,*
Roberta *(RKO 1935).*

'Mary's A Grand Old Name' and 'Yankee Doodle Boy'.

Until fairly recently, racial segregation in the movies forced great black artists to play minor roles in the history of the Hollywood musical. A dancer of the calibre of Bill 'Bojangles' Robinson found himself in the all-black *Stormy Weather* (1943) or as Shirley Temple's faithful servant in four Fox musicals, his deceptively easy-going tapping proving the ideal accompaniment to little Shirley's shuffling. Other black dancers such as Tip, Tap and Toe appeared in specialty numbers, as did the vertiginous footwork and splits of The Nicholas Brothers (Harold and Fayard). Their tumbling 'Be A Clown' number with Gene Kelly was cut from *The Pirate* when it was released in the Southern states of the USA.

At MGM in the 50s, the accent was on youth, and vigorous young dancers Tommy Rall, Bobby Van and Bob Fosse were given their chance. They appeared as Ann Miller's three suitors in *Kiss Me Kate*, Rall was one of the brothers in the exuberant *Seven Brides For Seven Brothers* (1954), Van hopped non-stop through the small town of *Small Town Girl* (1953), and Fosse flanked cheerful post-teenager Debbie Reynolds in bouncy, lightweight pictures, *The Affairs Of Dobie Gillis* (1953) and *Give A Girl A Break* (1952). The latter also starred Marge and Gower Champion, the husband-and-wife dancing team of the flashing legs and smiles.

ABOVE *A razzle-dazzle number from* All That Jazz *(Columbia-20th Century-Fox 1979), choreographed and directed by Bob Fosse, and continuing the tradition of glamorous dance musicals that he learnt on Broadway and at MGM in the 50s.*
RIGHT *Debbie Allen in Alan Parker's* Fame *(MGM 1980).*

Bob Fosse made his name as a Broadway choreographer-dancer. In Hollywood, he choreographed *The Pyjama Game* (1957) and *Damn Yankees* (1958), before directing *Sweet Charity* (1968) and *Cabaret* (1972). The semi-autobiographical *All That Jazz* (1979), is a two-hour cynical clinical razzle-dazzle production number about Fosse's own heart operation and his relations with his wife, mistress and daughter. The Fosse character (played by Roy Scheider) does not survive his meeting with Death, but male dancing on screen was given the kiss of life by the revelation of

John Travolta in *Saturday Night Fever* (1977). He came in on the crest of the disco-dancing craze which continued with the youthful verve of *Fame* (1980), *Can't Stop The Music* (1980) and *Flashdance* (1983), films that should be shown in seatless cinemas, giving the kids space to dance to them. The discotheque, with its strobe-lighting and tinsel atmosphere is the 80s equivalent of those sumptuous nightclubs of 30s musicals, sonic and scenic escapes from the drab realities outside. Although Travolta's range is narrow compared to Astaire or Kelly, he communicates the delight he has in his own vibrant steps. Dancing, according to Travolta in *Staying Alive* (1983), is 'all about body language' and he is loquacious in that regard.

Dance in the cinema satisfies the innate anarchy in us all. It allows us vicariously to shed our inhibitions, freeing us from social restraint and the restrictions of our bodies. At the drop of a top hat, we can begin to dance wherever we choose – in a lavish nightclub, on tables in a smart restaurant, in a crowded street, on top of The Empire State or The Eiffel Tower. We can dance on a mountain summit, from cloud to cloud, on the ceiling, or in the rain.

ABOVE AND LEFT *The disco-dancing craze gave a new impetus to the film musical in the 80s, from which new sparkling stars emerged. Jennifer Beals in* Flashdance *(Paramount 1983) and John Travolta, his body built up for his role in Sylvester Stallone's* Staying Alive *(Paramount 1983) were just a few of them. Travolta has the acrobatic exuberance of Gene Kelly and a strut reminiscent of Fred Astaire, but his flashing smile, cleft chin, blue eyes and his riveting dancing are all his own.*

ABOVE *Sheree North – 'Birth Of The Blues' from* The Best Things In Life Are Free *(1956).*   RIGHT *Marilyn Monroe in* Gentlemen Prefer Blondes *(1953).*

GENTLEMEN PREFER BLONDES

Her hair is blonde and curly,
Her curls are hurly-burly.
Her lips are pips,
I call her hips
Whirly and twirly.

Lyrics by Oscar Hammerstein II.
Sung by Mitzi Gaynor
in *South Pacific* (1958)

The opening number from *Blonde Venus* (1932) is a jungle setting where a group of swarthy chorines in Afro wigs are dancing to 'Hot Voodoo'. A huge, ugly gorilla enters and dances among them. Suddenly, it starts to unscrew its head to reveal the white face and blinding blonde hair of Marlene Dietrich. She steps out of the monkey-suit, shimmering in her blanched loveliness, her face radiating from a pool of light, rays streaming from her hair. She is the love goddess of the film's title – unreal, unattainable, desirable. The white madonna, the Anglo-Saxon ideal, the blonde sacred-whore was dreamed up by Hollywood believing the title of Anita Loos' 1925 novel 'Gentlemen Prefer Blondes', or as her narrator Lorelei Lee says, 'Gentlemen always seem to remember blondes.' From Jean Harlow to Marilyn Monroe, the blonde has been the centre of attraction and controversy. She didn't have to do very much, it was enough for her merely to exist. Twentieth Century-Fox built almost their entire musical output around the blonde. Blondes put the tinsel in Tinsel Town, and whether stars or chorus girls, they were an essential part of the cosmetic splendour of the musical.

Jean Harlow, the Platinum Blonde, only made one musical, but she created the mould from which others would be formed. She wore heavy make-up, pencil-thin eyebrows and clinging clothes. Harlow had to spend an hour in the make-up department every other day for the roots of her hair to be touched up. In *Reckless* (1935), she is recklessly dressed by Adrian, suggesting the nudity beneath the silver lamé. Skilful edit-

ABOVE *Marlene Dietrich, the* Blonde Venus *(Paramount 1932), shimmering in a darkest Africa number called 'Hot Voodoo' after miraculously emerging from a monkey suit.*

ing and the use of doubles, helped her to look competent in the dances and her singing was dubbed, yet her provocative sexuality showed why she was a star. Jean Harlow died suddenly and tragically of cerebral oedema in 1937. She was only 26.

Mae West, on the other hand, was 86 when she made her last film. Her first two, filmed when she was over 40, were campaigned against by The Catholic League Of Decency and were responsible for the setting up of the Hays Code. Although censorship toned down her erotic humour, her suggestive carnality survived. Mae West's well-upholstered figure was generally garbed in the extravagant fox furs, feather boas and huge hats of the 1890s. Sashaying with hands on hips, she personified and satirised female voluptuousness. The figure that 'launched a thousand hips', has been the inspiration of every drag artist since. She was not only photogenic and erotogenic, but had a delicious wit. (She wrote all her own material.) Some of her classic Wilde West epigrams included 'I used to be Snow White but I drifted', 'It's not the men in my life, it's the life in my

men that counts', and 'When I'm good I'm very good, but when I'm bad I'm better.' When a woman exclaims, 'Goodness! Where did you get those beautiful diamonds?', Mae replies in her languorous drawl, 'Goodness had nothing to do with it, dearie.'

Mae West could sing the blues as well as any black singer, and even attempted an operatic aria from 'Samson and Delilah' in *Goin' To Town* (1935). She squeezed as much innuendo as she could out of songs such as 'I Wonder Where My Easy Rider's Gone' from *She Done Him Wrong* (1933), and 'They Call Me Sister Honky Tonk' from *I'm No Angel* (1933). In *Klondike Annie* (1936), she emerges from behind veiled curtains in Eastern headgear and oriental gown, singing 'I'm An Occidental Woman In An Oriental Mood.' She was clothed by Paramount's premier designer Travis Banton. Ironically, Banton's uncle had prosecuted the cast of Mae West's play 'Sex' on Broadway for corrupting the morals of the young. She overlooked the incident and got Banton to design for her in Hollywood. When Banton left Paramount for Fox in 1937, the studio commissioned Italian-born

6*She's sizzling! She's explosive! She'll rock the nation with laughter! . . . This is lovely Jean Harlow's happiest role – as the vivacious, voluptuous bombshell of Hollywood who erupted so often she blew the lid off her own private life and loves!'*

MGM publicity for Bombshell (1933)

LEFT *The Platinum Blonde sexpot, Jean Harlow, being Reckless (MGM 1933) in a game attempt to sing and dance, but showing more leg than talent in her only musical.*
BELOW *Supreme hair-stylist Sydney Guilaroff attempting to reproduce the Harlow hairdo on Carroll Baker impersonating Harlow (Paramount 1965), but the original's special brand of raunchy blonde, glamour remained inimitable.*

'*It isn't what I do, but how I do it. It isn't what I say, but how I say it, and how I look when I do and say it.*'

Mae West

RIGHT '*It's better to be looked over than overlooked,*' *said Mae West, the mistress of sexual innuendo and a sashaying parody of a sex symbol, pictured here in a typically provocative pose from* She Done Him Wrong *(Paramount 1933).*
BELOW *A colour publicity still from* The Heat's On *(Columbia 1943) with the ever-seductive 51-year-old Mae West in her last picture before her 27-year-long retirement.*

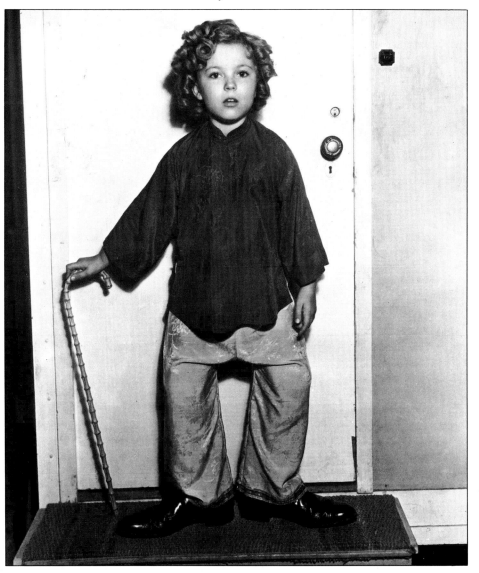

couturier Schiaparelli to do Mae West's costumes for *Every Day's A Holiday* (1937). However, Schiaparelli refused to go to America, so a dummy with Mae's ample measurements was sent to Paris. Unfortunately, when the creations arrived in Hollywood they were too small to accommodate Mae's curves. At great cost to Paramount, they had to be remodelled, but Schiaparelli adapted West's hour-glass figure from the dummy to a bottle of her latest perfume called 'Shocking'. Mae West is also the only film star who is in every English dictionary, having given her name during World War II to the airman's life-jacket.

Unlike Mae West, 'goodness' had everything to do with Shirley Temple's career, although they are not as different as would at first appear. Both had curly, blonde hair and dimples, both were teasers who had men falling over themselves to please them, both sang coquettishly. They were both a little freakish. Shirley Temple, the world's biggest and smallest star from 1934–1938, made her feature film debut singing 'Baby Take A Bow' in *Stand Up And Cheer* (1934) at the age of six. She was a bright-eyed, curly-topped, singing and dancing dimple whose cherubic chirpings and toddler's tappings were perfect antidotes to the adult preoccupation with the Depression. Her message was 'Be Optimistic' which she sang in her midget's voice in *Little Miss Broadway* (1938). Although she was all sunshine, she had her share of sass and could hold her own in a dance routine. Her first starring vehicle was *Little Miss Marker* (1934) based on a Damon Runyon short story. In the Runyon original, the tiny tot dances whenever she can 'holding her little short skirt up in her hands and showing a pair of white panties underneath.' Shirley dances a lot, but keeps her skirt decorously in place. Her biggest hits were 'On The Good Ship Lollypop' from *Bright Eyes* (1934) which describes a child's dream of a candy shop, and 'Animal Crackers In My Soup' from *Curly Top* (1935) sung at an orphanage during lunch as she skips between the tables and the kids beat time with their knives and forks. Already, at 10, she was beginning to show her age in *Just Around The Corner* (1938), and by the following year she was past her prime.

In *Stowaway* (1936), Shirley Temple displayed her considerable talents by impersonating Eddie Cantor, Al Jolson and Ginger Rogers dancing with a Fred Astaire doll. In the same film, a more mature Fox blonde sings Shirley a lullaby – 'Goodnight My Love' – on board ship. The blonde then turns away from childish things and dances to the same song with Robert Young on the romantic moonlit deck of the ship. Alice Faye had a little turned-up nose, pouting mouth and peroxide perm, was always superbly dressed and had a deep and mellow singing voice. She could belt out a song like 'He Ain't Got Rhythm' from *On The Avenue* (1937), or seduce with a tender ballad like 'You Say The Sweetest Things, Baby' from *Tin Pan Alley* (1940). She could act too, usually playing gutsy ladies who fall for the wrong guy; either darkly handsome Tyrone Power or John Payne. Alice Faye appeared mainly in opulent sagas that sometimes used historical backgrounds, but merely as pegs on which to hang a procession of familiar melodies such as *Alexander's Ragtime Band* (1938), *In Old Chicago* (1938), *Rose Of Washington Square* (1939), and *Hello, Frisco, Hello* (1943). Although they often stretched over a period of twenty years, the principals hardly aged a day.

Travis Banton, who had left Dietrich and Mae West at Paramount, designed the delicate costumes for Alice Faye in *Lillian Russell* (1940), set in that favourite period of the Fox musical, the Gay Nineties. However, Banton and Faye clashed on *That Night In Rio* (1941). She kept demanding flashier decoration on her costumes, arguing that Dietrich's were always

ABOVE *The multi-talented tiny tot Shirley Temple, the first and smallest of the Fox blondes, taking off Charlie Chaplin's Tramp, one of her many impersonations of her peers.*

RIGHT *A portrait of 20th Century-Fox's peroxide songbird Alice Faye, who embellished many a lavish period musical from 1936–1943.*

glittering. Banton informed her that Dietrich could carry it off but such clothes would only make Faye look vulgar. Head of production Darryl F. Zanuck reprimanded him for his rudeness to the star and Banton left Fox. Nevertheless, Alice Faye looked superb in the film, wearing a draped gold lamé evening gown covered in jewels. Gwen Wakeling, who had worked for her on many films, returned to design *Weekend In*

Havana (1941), cleverly disguising the star's pregnancy (she had married bandleader Phil Harris). Alice Faye retired from the screen in 1944, making a comeback 18 years later as Tom Ewell's wife in *State Fair* (1962), an undemanding role but played with her usual warmth.

Blondness, snow and ice combined in the whiter-than-white Fox entertainments starring Norwegian skating star Sonja Henie. She began skating at eight, was her country's champion at fourteen and won her first gold medal at the 1928 Olympics at St Moritz at the age of sixteen. Darryl Zanuck, no cheapskate, offered her $75,000 to make her screen debut in *One In A Million* (1937). She went on to skate through another seven sugar-coated, thin-ice musicals, perfectly suited to her uncomplicated and wholesome personality. For the skating sequences, the studio prop men sprayed a special kind of freezable paint over the ice to hide the refrigerator pipes underneath. Henie was self-conscious about her rather athletic legs and encased them in $35 sheer beige silk tights. Most of the pictures were set at a fashionable winter resort with either Don Ameche, Tyrone Power or John Payne literally falling for her. *My Lucky Star* (1938) finds Sonja working in a department store which is the setting for the 'Alice In Wonderland Ice Ballet' finale. The climax of *Sun Valley Serenade* (1941) was a ballet

RIGHT *Alice Faye recreating the atmosphere of 1871 as a music hall singer* In Old Chicago *(20th Century-Fox 1938), providing her own warmth before the Great Fire destroys the city.*

on black ice performed by Henie and company. On the last day of shooting, Henie fell and got covered in black dye. Instead of re-shooting, the director cut away just before the fall to her and John Payne skiing down a Sun Valley slope. The sequence of eight icicle-musicals in seven years, ended with *Wintertime* (1943). She hung her skates up for five years before appearing in her last American movie, *The Countess Of Monte Cristo* (1948). Sonja Henie, perhaps the most famous figure skater ever, died of leukemia in 1969.

Three-strip Technicolor began to be used more often from 1939. The process was invented by Dr Herbert Kalmus, whose wife, Natalie, was colour consultant on virtually every picture made in Technicolor until 1948. This was the finest period of colour in the history of Hollywood. Director Rouben Mamoulian commented, 'Up to now the movie picture industry has been like an artist only allowed to use pencil or charcoal. Now Technicolor has given us paints.' Technicolor during that era did not try to be natural, so films were visually richer, more exciting and more colourful than life. The musical was the perfect subject for this box of paints. Fox musicals did not have the creative talents of the MGM team, but they had the splashiest colour and the blondest of

blondes. Alice Faye emerged tentatively into the gaudy colour world in four of her many musicals, but her image on the retina remains a monochromatic one.

Betty Grable had been in movies for ten years before Fox and Technicolor discovered her. A former Goldwyn Girl, she was an ingenue in several RKO musicals, remembered mainly for knocking knees with Edward Everett Horton in *The Gay Divorcee* (1934). When Alice Faye was rushed to hospital with appendicitis, Grable was summoned from Broadway for the lead in *Down Argentine Way* (1940). This butter blonde with the peaches and cream complexion, full rose-red lips and beautiful long legs made a vivid impression. There followed over a dozen absurd, musical frolics with leggy Betty at their centre. Positively Houdini-like in their escapism, they were set in either the Gay 90s, exotic locales or wonderland holiday resorts. By her own admission, she could act 'just enough to get by', a phrase equally applicable to her dancing and singing, but Fox wrapped her up expertly in brightly coloured packages – just the thing to send the troops at the front. As a result, she became World War II's favourite pin-up. Over two million copies were sold of the famous pose of her in a white bathing suit looking seductively over her shoulder at the camera. If Mae West in proxy saved many an airman from drowning, then the army marched

BELOW *Norway's Sonja Henie, three times Olympic gold medal winner, brought her scintillating skating skills and blonde glamour to the black-ice ballet finale of* Sun Valley Serenade *(20th Century-Fox 1941).*

ABOVE *Alice Faye of the snub nose and throaty voice in Busby Berkeley's Technicolored extravaganza,* The Gang's All Here *(20th Century-Fox 1943).*

metaphorically on Betty's legs. The idea of the 'million-dollar legs' arose from a studio publicity stunt. They ran a phony contest to find the best starlet's legs in Hollywood and Betty won.

In *Down Argentine Way*, another of Hollywood's attempts to woo Latin America, Grable is an heiress who falls in love with Argentinian horse-breeder Don Ameche. The Argentinians spend their time singing, dancing and watching horse-races. *Moon Over Miami* (1941) finds her as a waitress in an open air hamburger

joint who comes into a legacy, and takes off for Florida where she shows as much leg as permissible. As *Sweet Rosie O'Grady* (1943), she sings 'My Heart Tells Me' in a bath tub, soaping her outstretched gams, and in *Billy Rose's Diamond Horseshoe* (1945), she plays a showgirl with 'a mink coat complex.' Inevitably, she starred in a film called *Pin Up Girl* (1944), one of her rare movies to refer to the war in Europe, ending with a military parade routine of WACS led by Betty Grable. Although her legs were insured for more than Fred Astaire's she made the mistake of not showing them in *The Shocking Miss Pilgrim* (1947) where, as a typist fighting for sexual equality in the business world of the Boston of 1874, she wore Puritan clothes down to the ground. Protests from thousands of fans forced Fox to call her next movie *Mother Wore Tights* (1947), the first of her four musicals with dancer Dan Dailey. Apart from the pastel apparel of the title, Betty managed to wear mid-calf slit skirts despite the film's turn-of-the-century setting and against the advice of designer Orry-Kelly. He refused to work with her again although, in this case, Betty knew best. Her fans obviously didn't give a fig for period authenticity as long as they could glimpse those legs, and *Mother Wore Tights* was one of her biggest box-office hits. Previously, Orry-Kelly was able to indulge his wildest costumier's fantasies in *The Dolly Sisters* (1945). Drenched in sumptuous colour, it offered kitschy

RIGHT *Bouncy blonde Betty Grable hoofing it with the Condos Brothers in a typically frivolous musical,* Moon Over Miami *(2oth Century-Fox 1941), with tropical palms representing the Florida landscape.*

production numbers including 'Darktown Strutters' Ball' with girls in black face and weird polka dot creations, and 'Powder, Lipstick And Rouge' with each chorus girl dressed as an item from a woman's make-up kit. Although the original Dolly Sisters were brunettes, Fox offered the public two blondes for the price of one. Unable to coax Alice Faye out of retirement, 19-year-old June Haver was given the role of Grable's younger sister.

June Haver made her screen debut as a hat-check girl in Busby Berkeley's *The Gang's All Here* (1943) and then went on to replay the Grable roles of a few years earlier. *Three Little Girls In Blue* (1946) was a remake of *Moon Over Miami*, and *I'll Get By* (1950) was an updated version of the Faye-Grable success *Tin Pan Alley*. She was even *The Daughter Of Rosie O'Grady* (1950). Less brassy and less energetic than Grable, Haver was a sweet, pretty, slightly anaemic blonde who, nevertheless, was the centrepiece of successful turn-of-the-century golden corn such as *Irish Eyes Are Smiling* (1944), *I Wonder Who's Kissing Her Now* (1947) and *Oh, You Beautiful Doll* (1949), the latter title perfectly describing her. In 1953, she left Hollywood to enter a convent with the intention of becoming a nun. She married Fred MacMurray instead. But a new Fox blonde was waiting in the wings to take over.

Born Norma Jean Baker in June 1926, the same month and year as June Haver, Marilyn Monroe nonetheless belongs to more permissive times. Billy Wilder described her as having 'breasts like granite and a brain like Swiss cheese, full of holes. Extracting a performance from her is like pulling teeth.' Yet she was magically transformed on screen into one of those rare celluloid creatures who create legends. Before reaching super stardom, she was chased lecherously by Groucho Marx in *Love Happy* (1950), mocked by George Sanders in *All About Eve* (1950) who intro-

ABOVE *June Haver, the girl in the gilded box, provided the inspiration behind the song* I Wonder Who's Kissing Her Now *(20th Century-Fox 1947), set in the Gay Nineties, the favourite period of frilly Fox musicals.*

LEFT *A vision of double blondeness as Betty Grable (left) and June Haver perform a leg-revealing number from* The Dolly Sisters *(20th Century-Fox 1945), a highly fictionalised account of the famous brunette sisters of turn-of-the-century vaudeville.*

OPPOSITE *The two 'little' girls from Little Rock, Marilyn Monroe and Jane Russell, in their spangled William Travilla costumes, posing with an understandably exultant Charles Coburn as diamond millionaire Sir Francis Beekman in* Gentlemen Prefer Blondes *(20th Century-Fox 1953).*

RIGHT *Marilyn Monroe in Irving Berlin's 'Tropical Heatwave' number from* There's No Business Like Show Business *(20th Century-Fox 1954).*
BELOW *Marilyn Monroe, between Donald O'Connor and Mitzi Gaynor, in the song 'Lazy' from* There's No Business Like Show Business.

duces her at a party as 'a graduate of the Copacabana School of Dramatic Art', and is aptly defined in *Monkey Business* (1952) as 'half-child, but not the half that shows.' Her undulating walk was first noticed in *Niagara* (1953), the tight, bright red dress clinging to her behind and diverting all eyes away from the grandeur of The Falls.

Marilyn Monroe made only three true musicals, but had songs in most of her other films. She sang in the loudest whisper, rotated rather than danced, but endowed her songs with a mixture of sugar and spice and wide-eyed wonderment at her own daring. She first revealed her comedic and musical skills in *Gentlemen Prefer Blondes* (1953) as Anita Loos' not-so-dumb diamond-digging blonde, Lorelei Lee. In an outfit of shocking pink satin, (created by her favourite designer William Travilla), and long black gloves bedecked with diamonds, she expounds the mercenary philosophy that 'Diamonds Are A Girl's Best Friend'. Even before the titles come up, Monroe and her dark-haired companion Jane Russell burst onto the screen in spangled red costumes singing 'Two Little Girls From Little Rock'. Travilla had to make sure that the dresses were so constructed as to allow the stars to shake a lot while their ample bosoms remained still. Marilyn's dimensions were successfully exaggerated by CinemaScope in *How To Marry A Millionaire* (1953), appearing with Betty Grable, now on her last legs in films. In *There's No Business*

MARILYN MONROE

Twentieth Century-Fox loved blondes and it loved musicals. So, a combination of the two sparked the moneymen, inspired the film-makers, and enthused the audiences. Fox had the lovely Alice Faye, the leggy Betty Grable. There was sweetly pretty June Haver, magical ice-skater Sonja Henie, and ... Marilyn Monroe.

Compared with those others, Marilyn was not in the same league of hoofing and singing excellence. But what she *did* have was personality, a way of projection that had nothing to do with that eloquent bosom. But a good deal to do with wanting to be noticed – by the camera lens, if nothing else more human came along. She infiltrated that quality into the role of the gold-digging Lorelei Lee in *Gentlemen Prefer Blondes* (1953), and the brilliant and raucous *Some Like It Hot* (1959) saw her as another pouting siren – both wonderfully comedic performances, and softened by her breathless vulnerability.

Her last musical towards the end of that too brief life, *Let's Make Love* (1960), had her much publicised as taking the title too literally with co-star Yves Montand. It was pretty much of a pretty disaster, but then so much was disastrous around Marilyn just before she died so tragically in California.

So what did she bring to musicals? She brought to musicals the quality that is best defined by saying her initials. M.M. equals mm....!

ABOVE *An early publicity still for* All About Eve *(20th Century-Fox, 1950), in which the unknown starlet found herself in company with no less than George Sanders and Bette Davis.*

ABOVE RIGHT *In company with the dark-haired and sultry Jane Russell, Marilyn hoofs it as Lorelei Lee, Anita Loos's immortal gold-digger in* Gentlemen Prefer Blondes *(20th Century-Fox, 1953).*

RIGHT *In Billy Wilder's classic comedy,* Some Like It Hot *(United Artists, 1959), Jack Lemmon and Tony Curtis don drag and join an all-girl band to escape pursuing gangsters. The provocative presence of fellow-musician Marilyn almost causes their cover to collapse.*

LEFT *The not-yet distinctive glamour of early Marilyn, photographic model and starlet. The inset is more Norma Jean Barber – Marilyn's real name – than the Monroe familiar to moviegoers.*

ABOVE *Life at the top begins to take its toll ... a later photograph displays a coarse edge to Marilyn's ultimately fatal vulnerability.*

'*The trouble with censors is they worry if a girl has cleavage. They ought to worry if she hasn't any.*'

Marilyn Monroe

Like Show Business (1954), she drives Donald O'Connor to drink and men crazy with three Irving Berlin numbers, 'Lazy', 'Heat Wave' and 'After You Get What You Want You Don't Want It', her image filling the wide screen bountifully, against the dominant garish mauves of Fox films of the 50s.

In the vast open CinemaScope spaces of Otto Preminger's *River Of No Return* (1954), she is asked by little Tommy Rettig, 'What's Opera?' She modestly replies, 'It's music. Very high-toned and fancy. Not like mine.' She demonstrates this by singing three ditties during the film, first in a red dress, then in a green one, before slipping into jeans and a more wholesome image. Monroe sings two zippy 20s numbers, 'Runnin' Wild' (with ukelele) and 'I Wanna Be Loved By You' in *Some Like It Hot* (1959). As Sugar Kane, she is the genuine feminine article in contrast to the parody of womanhood portrayed by Jack Lemmon and Tony Curtis in drag, a blonde and brunette not unlike Monroe and Russell in *Gentlemen Prefer Blondes* except the brunette (Curtis), in this case, is the sensitive one. Her three songs in her last musical *Let's Make Love* (1960) – 'My Heart Belongs To Daddy', 'Specialisation' and the title number, bring verve to the tired goings on around her. She was to complete one more film, *The Misfits* (1961), before her death from a drug overdose in 1962. The Monroe doctrine that 'sex is part of nature and I go along with nature' was later sadly qualified by her comment that 'a sex symbol becomes a thing. I hate being a thing.'

Twentieth Century-Fox had other blondes ready to take over from Marilyn, only to prove there could be no substitute. Jayne Mansfield showed a certain sensitivity behind the breast fetishism imposed upon her. Her big-bosomed, dumb-blondness was mercilessly sent up in Frank Tashlin's *The Girl Can't Help It* (1957). It featured a dozen rock and roll stars and Mansfield's rock and roll walk. When she swings down the street, a block of ice held by an iceman turns to steam, milk boils in a bottle, and a man's spectacles crack. Tashlin's crude humour is demonstrated when Mansfield enters her apartment carrying two milk bottles suggestively in front of each breast. 'She's just a girl,' says Tom Ewell to a precocious 12-year-old newsboy. 'If she's a girl, then I don't know what my sister is,' he replies. For her role as a singer in a Soho strip joint in *Too Hot To Handle* (1960), she had to have more sequins sewn on her mainly transparent dress in order to get past the censor. Jayne Mansfield was tragically killed in a horrendous motor accident on her way to a TV studio in 1967.

Although Fox had the monopoly on blondes,

RIGHT *Pleasurable prettiness was provided by minor musicals such as* Ain't Misbehavin' *(Universal 1951) with Piper Laurie (centre), between Dani Crayne (left) and Mamie Van Doren, doing the Charleston.*

LEFT *Breathless, bosomy blonde Jayne Mansfield, whose build was the butt of cruel cracks in Frank Tashlin's* The Girl Can't Help It *(20th Century-Fox 1957), seemed to take the sending up in good fun.*
ABOVE *The flounces and frills in* The Sheriff Of Fractured Jaw *(20th Century-Fox 1958) were supplied by Jayne Mansfield as a saloon hostess, with Connie Francis providing her singing voice.*

Warner Bros. had *the* blonde singer of the 50s. Doris Mary Anne von Kappelhof, alias Doris Day, was an antidote to the rather brassy blondes and mammary mania at Fox. Whereas Monroe was the girl downtown, Doris Day was the archetypal girl-next-door. She had short buttercup hair, a sunny smile, a honey voice, and as many scruples as freckles, prompting Groucho Marx to say, 'I've been around so long, I can remember Doris Day before she was a virgin.' She came out of the big band boom of the 40s, and was box-office magic right through the 60s, although her last musical was the heavy *Jumbo* (1962).

Most of her pictures at Warner Bros. were nostalgic candy-floss vehicles named after song titles. She co-starred with clean-cut, well-built baritone Gordon MacRae in four of them. *On Moonlight Bay* (1951) and its sequel *By The Light Of The Silvery Moon* (1953) were idyllic small-town musicals, faded copies of MGM's superior *Meet Me In St Louis* (1944), but injected with her freshness and vitality. Although her hygienic good-looks were exploited, she had her share of glamour in *Tea For Two* (1950), *Lullaby Of Broadway* (1951), *I'll See You In My Dreams* (1951) and *April In Paris* (1952).

In her first film for MGM, *Love Me Or Leave Me* (1955), a biopic of torch singer Ruth Etting, Doris Day was splendidly attired by Helen Rose, the studio's leading designer of the 50s. The part was intended for Ava Gardner, but she refused to have her singing dubbed as it had been in *Show Boat* (1951). Day gave one of her meatiest performances as the singer who was helped to stardom by bootlegging gangster Martin 'The Gimp' Snyder (James Cagney). As most of the principals were still alive, MGM paid each an undisclosed sum for the rights to use their names in the film. Ruth Etting, while obviously pleased with Day's interpretation, denied she had ever been a dance-hall girl as depicted in the film, claiming it was only a way of getting in the song, 'Ten Cents A Dance'. Doris Day sings a dozen other ballads, anachronistically scored by Percy Faith, including 'Shakin' The Blues Away', 'You Made Me Love You' and 'Mean To Me'. In contrast, Day remained grimy throughout *Calamity Jane* (1953), only emerging at the end from the chrysalis of tomboy-hood into a butterfly of femininity

LEFT *For her role as nightclub singer Ruth Etting in* Love Me Or Leave Me *(MGM 1955), Doris Day, pictured here singing 'Shaking The Blues Away', was given the Metro-Helen Rose glamour treatment.*
BELOW *As the buckskin-wearing, swearing, sharpshooting Calamity Jane (Warner Bros. 1953) who 'Just Blew In From The Windy City', Doris Day displayed the gutsy side of her talent.*

RIGHT *Blonde Bombshell Betty Hutton in the greatest role of her career as Annie Oakley in* Annie Get Your Gun *(MGM 1950), a reward for throwing herself about in numerous noisy musicals at Paramount.*
OPPOSITE *Betty Hutton looking uncharacteristically demure as Texas Guinan, speakeasy hostess of the prohibition era, in* Incendiary Blonde *(Paramount 1945).*

in order to charm Howard Keel as 'Wild Bill' Hickock, her 'Secret Love'. The Oscar-winning song is warbled leaning against a tree, then on horseback, and at the top of a hill at the top of her voice. *Calamity Jane* was her compensation for not getting the coveted lead in MGM's *Annie Get Your Gun* (1950) which gave Betty Hutton – taking over from a nerve-shattered, drug-addicted Judy Garland – her greatest chance.

Jitterbug and Jive, those epileptic dances of the 40s, produced frenetic, ear-splitting female vocalists like Cass Daley, Judy Canova, Martha Raye and blonde bombshell Betty Hutton. Hutton worked almost

BELOW *Dimpled, blonde ex-Goldwyn Girl Virginia Mayo, who often appeared in the sweet dreams of Danny Kaye, seen here entertaining in her limited but attractive way in a couple of Warner Bros. musicals.*

exclusively for Paramount, knocking herself out in explosive numbers such as 'Murder He Says', full of hepcat vocabulary, from *Happy Go Lucky* (1943), and 'I'm A Square In The Social Circle' from *The Stork Club* (1945). She appeared in two colour biopics which completely lacked any sense of period – *Incendiary Blonde* (1945) about Texas Guinan, nightclub hostess of the 20s, and *The Perils Of Pauline* (1947), based on the life of silent screen serial queen Pearl White, in which Hutton sings 'Poppa Don't Preach To Me' with her usual noisy gusto. Her teaming up with Fred Astaire in *Let's Dance* (1950) was a tasteless chalk and cheese soufflé. Betty Hutton was quite pretty when not distorting her face and sometimes offered a quieter ballad with tenderness.

Virginia Mayo was the picture of blonde prettiness. She graduated from the ranks of Goldwyn Girls to become Danny Kaye's dream girl in four Goldwyn Technicolored musicals in the 40s. Her dancing was unmemorable and she hardly differed from role to role, whether as a sweet librarian to Kaye's bookworm in *Wonder Man* (1945), or hep nightclub singer (dubbed by Jerri Sullivan) whose songs are studied by musicologist Kaye in *A Song Is Born* (1948), but she was eminently decorative. At Warners in the 50s, she starred in tepid but tuneful trivia such as *Painting The Clouds With Sunshine* (1951), an old Gold-diggers plot warmed up, and *She's Working Her Way Through College* (1952) with Mayo as a stripper who gets an education from Professor Ronald Reagan, substantiating the idea that 'blondes have more fun.'

. . . But gentlemen marry brunettes. It was a Hollywood convention that in an eternal triangle, the

'*Sometimes the photographers would pose me in a low-necked nightgown and tell me to bend down and pick up a couple of pails. They were not shooting the pails. Or else they would tell me to jump up and down in bed, in a nightgown while they shot from above and below. I didn't realise what they were doing. I was as green as grass.*

Jane Russell on the taking of publicity shots for her first film in 1941.

RIGHT *Dark-haired beauty Debra Paget in her Naughty Nineties costume from* Stars And Stripes Forever *(20th Century-Fox 1952), anachronistically appearing as a fifties calender girl for this publicity still.*

wife should be dark and the other woman blonde. In the main, it was a need for visual contrast that dictated the casting. In *Gentlemen Prefer Blondes*, it is the blonde Marilyn who settles for a gold band rather than diamonds, while brunette Jane Russell resists Monroe's advice 'to find happiness and stop having fun.' The more extrovert Russell sings 'Ain't There Anybody Here For Love?' in a ship's gymnasium to a team of muscle men. The question in the song is rhetorical as they are plainly more interested in their own bodies than in what she has to offer. (Muscles are a boy's best friend?) Later, Jane in a blonde wig, joins Marilyn for a

duet. It was Howard Hughes, an ex-aircraft engineer, who designed Russell's cantilever bra for his production *The Outlaw* (1943), the publicity line being 'There are two good reasons why men should see this picture.' Russell's bust in 3D was the gimmick for *The French Line* (1954), in which she wears a strapless leotard embroidered with red sequins and jet, causing RKO to get into difficulties with the censorious Hays Office. Jane Russell appeared as a pistol packin' mama in two Bob Hope western-musicals, *The Paleface* (1948) and *Son Of Paleface* (1952). In the latter, while Hope ogles Russell suggestively singing 'What A

Night For A Wing-Ding', cowboy Roy Rogers hardly blinks. 'What's the matter?' asks Hope. 'Don't you like girls?' 'I'll stick to horses, mister,' the Trigger-happy Rogers replies.

However, Bob Hope's favourite brunette was sultry, good-humoured Dorothy Lamour, the bone of contention between Hope and Bing Crosby in six Road movies. Born Dorothy Kaumeyer, she was a nightclub singer before she was put into a sarong for her first film, *The Jungle Princess* (1936), a garment that was associated with her throughout her career. If Betty Grable was the girl back home for the GIs, Lamour was the girl they dreamed of meeting on an island in the South Pacific. Her tropical island epics apart, she sang rather languidly through over two dozen Paramount musicals, including *The Fleet's In* (1942) and *And The Angels Sing* (1944) in direct contrast to effervescent co-star Betty Hutton. She is a saloon singer in *Lulu Belle* (1948), and she plays an Irish girl who passes herself off as a French star in *Slightly French* (1949), even attempting the Can-Can

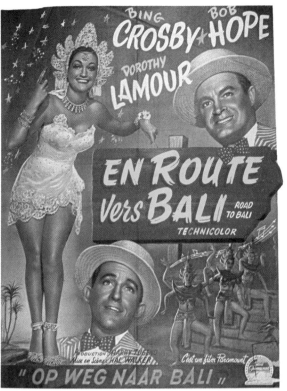

LEFT *A poster proving that Bob Hope, Bing Crosby and Dorothy Lamour's travels broke all language barriers. Certainly Miss Lamour's shapely figure needed no translation.*

LEFT *Susan Hayward smiling and miming to the voice of Jane Froman in* With A Song In My Heart *(20th Century-Fox 1952).* BELOW *Mitzi Gaynor, a cute, sprightly dancer-singer with a little turned-up nose, was an attractive addition to fifties musicals before retiring from the screen in 1960.*

RIGHT *Ravishing Rita Hayworth accompanied here by the prolific cinematic dance director Hermes Pan, in a number from the Gay Nineties spectacular* My Gal Sal *(20th Century-Fox 1942).*

BELOW *There were no complaints when Rita Hayworth played a double role in* Cover Girl *(Columbia 1944), a film that indulged in the musical's obsession with the turn-of-the-century so that dress designers could indulge in more fantasy than World War II fashions permitted.*

in a number called 'Fifi From The Folies Bergere.'

Flickering like a red flame among the blondes and brunettes, was the loveliness of Rita Hayworth. *My Gal Sal* (1942) was a ravishing Technicolor showcase for her, revolutionary for Fox in not using one of their blondes. In lavish period dresses designed by Gwen Wakeling, Hayworth dances and sings through this Gay Nineties piece. For *Cover Girl* (1944), Columbia's first Technicolor movie, Wakeling was one of three designers. Rita's first encounter with French-born costumier Jean Louis was on the 'London-can-take-it' wartime musical *Tonight And Every Night* (1945). As she was pregnant at the time, the more revealing numbers were moved to the beginning of shooting when she could still wear a bare midriff costume, while at the end she's in a flowing cloak. Jean Louis designed the black strapless gown for her in *Gilda* (1946) in which she sings (with Anita Ellis' voice), 'Put The Blame On Mame', while peeling off her long black gloves in a symbolic striptease. She was later to say, 'Every man I knew had fallen in love with Gilda and wakened with me.' As *Salome* (1953), she strips as far as the fourth veil, dancing to save the head of John the Baptist, in this version. Although her singing was always dubbed, she was an alluring dancer and it was appropriate that she should play Terpsichore, the goddess of dance, in the colourful fantasy, *Down To Earth* (1947).

The limpid, over-enunciated coloratura soprano voice emanating from Julie Andrews' ample mouth, is

ABOVE *A dancer of considerable ability, Rita Hayworth was convincing as Terpsichore, the Muse of Dance in* Down To Earth *(Columbia 1947), which contained some 'heavenly' sequences.*
LEFT *Rita Hayworth at the peak of her allurement as* Gilda *(Columbia 1946), pictured here in a strapless gown designed by Jean Louis for this romantic film noir.*

ABOVE *Julie Andrews as the 'supercalifragilisticexpialidocious' nanny in her remarkable screen debut as* Mary Poppins *(Buena Vista 1964), frolicking through a cartoon landscape with Dick Van Dyke to the amusement of the children, Karen Dotrice and Matthew Garber.*

RIGHT *In an attempt to escape her 'wholesome' image, Julie Andrews wore a badge which read 'Mary Poppins is a junkie'. She then cropped her hair, put on men's clothes, and teased her way through* Victor/Victoria *(U.I.P. 1982).*

her own. She entered films as the apotheosis of English nannyhood in *Mary Poppins* (1964), went on to play a singing governess in the chocolate box-office hit, *The Sound Of Music* (1965) and, despite frantic efforts to change the colour of her hair and her insipid image, she remains essentially a girl guide in attractive costumes. In bobbed brown hair and flapper's frock, her English rosiness blossomed in *Thoroughly Modern Millie* (1967), an over-cute lampoon of the 20s, but she was miscast as Gertrude Lawrence in the old-hat biopic *Star!* (1968), and did a coy striptease in *Darling Lili* (1969). As a woman pretending to be a man playing a woman in the gay (in both senses) musical comedy, *Victor-Victoria* (1982), she looked convincing in short-cropped red hair and male suit, but lacked the sexual ambiguity that Marlene Dietrich in top hat and tails brought to her singing of 'Quand L'Amour Meurt' in *Morocco* (1930). In supposed contrast to Julie's androgyny, Leslie Anne Warren is the stereotyped dumb blonde who squeakily sings 'Chicago, Illinois' with chorus girls. Air from below lifts their dresses like Marilyn Monroe's as she stood over the subway grating in *The Seven Year Itch* (1955). As a logical extension of this, the girls' dresses are blown off completely.

'That gentlemen prefer blondes is due to the fact that, apparently, pale hair, delicate skin and an infantile expression represent the very apex of a frailty which every man longs to violate' wrote the psychologist Alexander King. Whatever the explanation, male chauvinist or otherwise, and despite the array of brunettes and red-heads in the movies, it is the blonde who is characterised as the exemplar of the Hollywood glamour girl.

ABOVE *Banjo-eyed, corn-craking Carol Channing in one of her rare screen appearances, bringing humour and pezazz to* Thoroughly Modern Millie *(Universal 1967).*

LEFT *Real-life sisters Catherine Deneuve (the blonde) and Françoise Dorléac were two of* The Young Girls Of Rochefort *(Warner Bros. 1967), Jacques Demy's love letter from France to the Hollywood musical. Dorléac died in a car accident at the age of 25 in the same year.*

ABOVE *Kathryn Grayson and Howard Keel* in Show Boat *(1951)*.   RIGHT *22-year-old Judy Garland in* Meet Me In St. Louis *(1944), sings 'The Trolley Song'*.

THAT'S ENTERTAINMENT

A show that is really a show,
Sends you out with a kind of a glow,
And you say as you go on your way,
That's entertainment.
A song that is winging along,
Or a dance with a touch of romance,
Is the art that appeals to the heart,
That's entertainment.

Lyrics by Howard Dietz
from *The Band Wagon* (1953).

How odd of MGM to have chosen a roaring lion for its logo to introduce its silent pictures in 1924, unless they had foreseen the coming of sound. MGM was to become the King of studios in the Hollywood jungle and Leo's roar would be heard as a prelude to the greatest film musicals. MGM's glamour factory boasted of having 'more stars than there are in the heavens', its rather pompous motto being Ars Gratia Artis (Art for art's sake). Working for the sake of the art of musicals, was a peerless creative group of directors, designers, musicians, writers, performers and dance directors, led by producer Arthur Freed, the Diaghilev of the musical. The team became known as The Freed Unit, creating a distinguished and distinctive MGM style of musical movie.

The films that burst from The Freed Unit were the culmination of all previous techniques and experiments of the fifteen or so years since Al Jolson uttered the immortal words, 'Wait a minute, wait a minute. You ain't heard nothin' yet...' in *The Jazz Singer* (1927). The new look and direction came from the integration of musical numbers into the film's narrative theme, so that song, dance and music no longer punctuated the story, but actually advanced the plot. By a discriminating use of colour to suit the appropriate mood, (unlike the slap-dash, garish Fox colours), and highly stylised sets, a world was created in which the characters were moved to express their emotions through song and dance. Therefore, it is perfectly logical that three sailors in *On The Town* (1949) should manifest their joy at a day's leave in New York by literally singing the

ABOVE *MGM's top romantic male star Clark Gable rehearsed for six weeks for his three-minute song-and-dance, 'Puttin' On The Ritz', as hoofer Harry Van with his all-girl troupe in* Idiot's Delight *(1939)*.

same pace. The pulsating 'On The Atchison, Topeka And The Santa Fe' from *The Harvey Girls* (1946), is a melodic welcome sung by the citizens of Sandrock, New Mexico, echoed by the train driver, fireman, conductor and mostly girl passengers. When they alight, they introduce themselves in song, and the number ends with the crowds moving alongside the departing train, imitating its shuttling movements.

An emphasis on dance also characterised the Freed musicals, many of them containing full-length ballets, loosely connected to the story. The final ballet in *An American In Paris* (1951), is Gene Kelly's daydream of his lost love and a celebration of the city that has meant so much to him. 'The Pirate Ballet' from *The Pirate* (1948) is Judy Garland's romantic projection of her belief that Gene Kelly's ham actor is really Black Macoco, the bloodthirsty buccaneer whom she secretly desires. Sometimes as in the 'A Day In New York' ballet from *On The Town*, it merely mirrors the plot of the movie; or in *Singin' In The Rain* (1952), the narrative 'Broadway Ballet' is a semi-pastiche of a similar 30s number.

praises of that 'wonderful town'; or that a girl could sing of how she met the boy she loves on a turn-of-the-century streetcar in *Meet Me In St. Louis* (1944), on that same clang-clanging trolley. These single musical numbers move through a variety of locales, instead of keeping to one specific area. The sailors begin to sing 'New York, New York' at the docks and end the song at the Empire State Building, after taking in the sights; 'The Trolley Song', sung by Judy Garland and all the other passengers, moves along with the vehicle at the

Departing from hurried, hackneyed screenplays, thin narrative threads on which to hang the numbers, Freed's MGM musicals provided literate scripts which carried as much weight as the songs and dances that grew out of them. For the first time, musicals were seen as a whole and not as a fragmentary series of delights. Many of the non-musical moments are as

RIGHT *The spectacular arrival of 'The Atchison, Topeka And The Santa Fe', welcomed in typical MGM style in George Sidney's* The Harvey Girls *(1946)*.

memorable as the routines. Their tone is self-aware, sophisticated and gently satirical. *The Band Wagon* (1953) wittily inverts the clichés of the genre, also taking side swipes at classical ballet, 'high-brow' theatre and dime novels. When Oscar Levant says, 'Gosh, with all this raw talent around, why can't us kids get together and put on ourselves a show', he is taking off dialogue in Arthur Freed's own early productions with the youthful Mickey Rooney and Judy Garland.

Arthur Freed was born Arthur Grossman in Charleston, South Carolina in 1894. He began his career as a song plugger for a music publisher and later appeared with the Marx Brothers in vaudeville. Freed started writing songs and was hired as a lyricist by MGM in 1929 as the sound era dawned, and with Nacio Herb Brown, wrote 'Singin' In The Rain', 'You Were Meant For Me' and 'You Are My Lucky Star', among other memorable evergreens. Anxious to become a producer, he persuaded Louis B. Mayer to buy the rights of L. Frank Baum's famous children's book, 'The Wizard Of Oz.' Mayer did so, but entrusted the project to Mervyn LeRoy, making Freed associate producer.

The Wizard Of Oz (1939) required 29 sound stages, 65 sets, hundreds of costumes by Adrian, 150 singing and dancing midgets, and spectacular special effects, making it the most successful children's musical

fantasy ever made. The first scenes in sepia represent the drab reality of little Dorothy's life on a Kansas farm, a violent contrast with the colour of the land 'over the rainbow' in which she later finds herself. The film and Dorothy open up a door on a Technicolored dreamland of a yellow brick road, magical ruby slippers, the Emerald City of Oz, and the horse of a different colour. (The horse was to have been painted, but the S.P.C.A. objected. Jelly powder was used, which the horse kept licking, causing a constant need

ABOVE *Dance was a dominant force in the Arthur Freed-produced MGM musicals, and the ten-minute 'Broadway Ballet', featuring Gene Kelly and Cyd Charisse,* in Singin' In The Rain *(1952) demonstrated this admirably. 'I can't quite visualize it,' says producer Millard Mitchell in the movie.*

LEFT *Superb Cyd Charisse as ballet star Gaby in* The Band Wagon *(1953), making an impressive entrance with her corps de ballet. In the audience, an anxious Fred Astaire, set to dance with her in a Broadway show, worries that she may be taller than him.*

RIGHT *Arthur Freed (left), supremo of MGM musicals, on the set with formally attired Fred Astaire and Ginger Rogers during the making of their reunion picture, the Technicolor* The Barkleys Of Broadway *(1949).*

WHEN Berkeley first worked with her, he was driven half-crazy by her apparent inability to listen to anything he was saying. He was partial to giving elaborate instructions and was very put out when Judy stared off into space when he was talking to her. He would then become incensed and scream... whereupon Judy would repeat his instructions word for word, unable to figure out what had provoked his outburst.

ABOVE *Christopher Finch in* Rainbow *a biography of Judy Garland.*

RIGHT *Judy Garland with 'natural' make-up and hairdo as Dorothy in* The Wizard Of Oz *(1939), holding Toto in her arms and gaining support from tinselled Glinda, the Good Witch, played by Billie Burke, the ex-Mrs Florenz Ziegfeld.*

for reapplications.) In her black and white world, Judy Garland as Dorothy wistfully sings 'Somewhere Over The Rainbow', the song that would forever be associated with her. She was later to comment, 'It is so symbolic of everyone's dream and wish that I'm sure that's why people get tears in their eyes when they hear it. It's the song that's closest to my heart.' Yet the MGM brass thought the song slowed down the action, and had it cut from the picture; Freed's protestations got it reinstated permanently. Initially, Mayer wanted Shirley Temple for the role of Dorothy, but when Fox wouldn't release her, Freed insisted they try 16-year-old Judy Garland. Mayer thought Judy terribly plain, called her his 'monkey' and denied her any glamour in her teens. She was growing rapidly and had to have her breasts bound and her dresses carefully designed to give her the appearance of the 12-year-old Dorothy. George Cukor, the second of four directors on the picture (he only stayed a few days!), got rid of the blonde wig and doll's make-up she had been given, presumably to imitate Temple, and stressed the character's naturalness. He was right, and the film, finally directed by Victor Fleming, made Judy Garland into a star.

Encouraged by the triumph of *The Wizard Of Oz*,

LEFT *The major songwriters of MGM musicals, composer Nacio Herb Brown (at piano) and lyricist Arthur Freed (producer from 1939), whose songs include 'Singin' In The Rain', 'All I Do Is Dream Of You' and 'You Are My Lucky Star'.*

THE HARVEY GIRLS is a perfect demonstration of what Hollywood can do with its vast resources when it wants to be really showy. A skeleton of a horse opera has been clothed sumptuously with pretty girls, period sets and costumes, brawls and conflagrations...

ABOVE *Howard Barnes in the New York Herald Tribune 1946.*

LEFT *Mickey Rooney, Judy Garland, and Tommy Dorsey and His Orchestra in* Girl Crazy *(1943), the last vehicle built around the Judy-Mickey team. Naturally, the kids put on a show to end the movie, which included 'one hundred beautiful gals'.*

RIGHT *A colour publicity still of Judy Garland and Mickey Rooney in the early forties. They both – particularly Rooney – look more than their respective ages at the time.*

Louis B. Mayer decided to set up a musical unit at MGM, with Arthur Freed at its head. Freed immediately persuaded Busby Berkeley to come over from Warners to Metro to direct three of his first productions, the Rooney-Garland vehicles, *Babes In Arms* (1939), *Strike Up The Band* (1940), and *Babes On Broadway* (1941). Although Freed got him to tone down his choreographic fantasies and concentrate more on the young stars, Berkeley continued to think big. The crunch came with *Girl Crazy* (1943). Roger Edens, associate producer and musical adapter commented, 'I wanted the numbers rhythmic and simply staged; but Berkeley got his big ensembles and trick cameras into it again, plus a lot of girls in western

outfits, ... and people cracking whips, firing guns ... and cannons going off all over my arrangement and Judy's voice. Well, we shouted at each other, and I said, there wasn't enough room on the lot for both of us.' Freed dismissed Berkeley from the picture. The 'Babes' movies had a freshness and vigour, but were still part of the old 'backstage' musical tradition. Both Freed and Garland wanted to move into new territory, and they soon found the director who was to realise their dreams.

Vincente Minnelli had worked on the New York stage as a designer and director of ballets and musical comedies before Freed asked him to come to Hollywood in 1941. Minnelli was given two years of

training in film technique, staging isolated numbers for Judy Garland in two of the Berkeley musicals as a prelude to directing his first film, the all-black morality-musical, *Cabin In The Sky* (1943). By creating flesh-and-blood characters in the dream-built story of the battle for a soul between De Lawd and Lucifer, it transcends negro stereotypes and allows Lena Horne, Ethel Waters, Duke Ellington and Eddie 'Rochester' Anderson to give of their best. Minnelli's musicals conjure up a sophisticated, semi-real world of superb colour, stylish sets and costumes. A knowledge and taste for art and design imbue his films. *Yolanda And The Thief* (1945) is drenched in exotic colours and Fred Astaire dreams himself dancing in a Dali-Yves Tanguy landscape. The ballet finale of *An American In Paris* is a series of *tableaux dansantes* based on French Impressionist and Post-Impressionist paintings with Gene Kelly at one moment in the posture of Lautrec's 'Chocolat'. Cyd Charisse dances against a Chagall-like backdrop in *The Band Wagon*, and in the same film Fred Astaire's hotel room is bedecked with originals by Degas, Modigliani and Renoir, which are finally sold to finance a show. ('Those fellows loved the theatre,' explains Fred.) However, the first real masterpiece of

ABOVE *A host of brilliant black entertainers got the rare chance to display their skills at length in the all-black musical* Cabin In The Sky *(1943), the auspicious debut movie of director Vincente Minnelli.*

LEFT *Vincente Minnelli was given ample scope to express his taste for decorative fantasy in this dream ballet from* Yolanda And The Thief *(1946), with Fred Astaire and green-eyed, red-haired Lucille Bremer (on ground).*

115

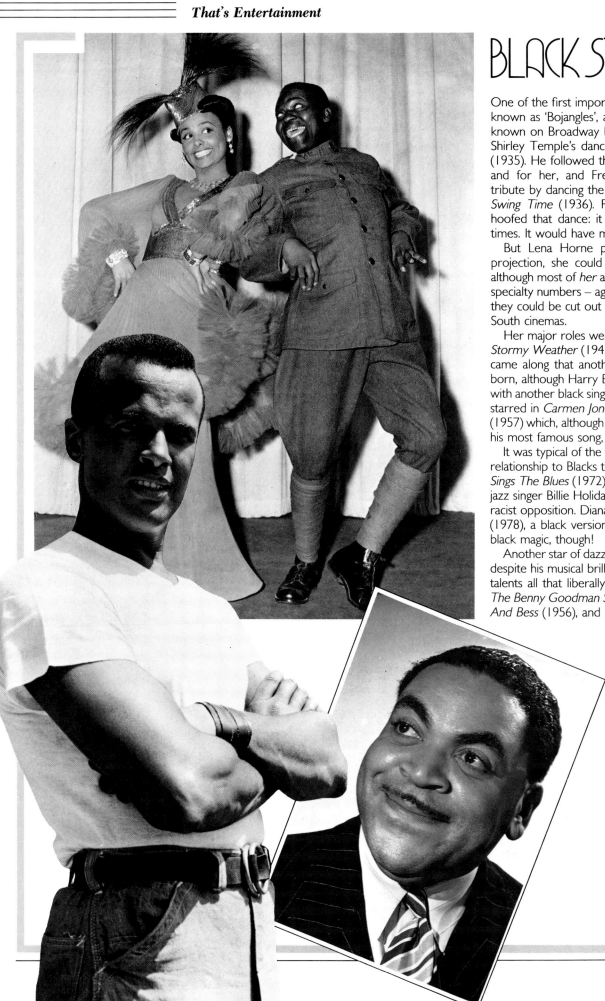

BLACK STARS

One of the first important black stars was Bill Robinson, known as 'Bojangles', a dancer and choreographer well known on Broadway before he went to Hollywood as Shirley Temple's dancing partner in *The Little Colonel* (1935). He followed that with four more films with her and for her, and Fred Astaire paid him black-faced tribute by dancing the 'Bojangles Of Harlem' number in *Swing Time* (1936). Robinson himself could not have hoofed that dance: it was not in the character of the times. It would have meant his being part of the story.

But Lena Horne proved that, in terms of sexual projection, she could be the equal of any white girl, although most of *her* appearances in MGM movies were specialty numbers – again isolated – but this time so that they could be cut out when being shown in racist Deep South cinemas.

Her major roles were in *Cabin In The Sky* (1943) and *Stormy Weather* (1943), but it was not until Diana Ross came along that another black star of that calibre was born, although Harry Belafonte had emerged for a time with another black singer, Dorothy Dandridge – they co-starred in *Carmen Jones* (1954) – and *Island In The Sun* (1957) which, although not a musical, was responsible for his most famous song, 'Island In The Sun.'

It was typical of the way musicals had changed in their relationship to Blacks that Miss Ross's first film was *Lady Sings The Blues* (1972), a socially-concerned affair about jazz singer Billie Holiday who herself encountered much racist opposition. Diana Ross's next movie was *The Wiz* (1978), a black version of *The Wizard Of Oz* – hardly black magic, though!

Another star of dazzling vitality is Sammy Davis Jr who, despite his musical brilliance on stage, has not spread his talents all that liberally on film, although he began with *The Benny Goodman Story* (1956) and also made *Porgy And Bess* (1956), and *Sweet Charity* (1969).

TOP LEFT *The beautiful and gifted Lena Horne is partnered by the great Bill 'Bojangles' Robinson in their opening number from 20th Century-Fox's* Stormy Weather *(1943).*
LEFT *The illustrious composer and jazz pianist, 'Fats' Waller. The numerous durable standards he wrote include 'Ain't Misbehavin', the title of a 1970s Broadway hit which paid tribute to his work. Waller made several film appearances, notably in* Stormy Weather.
FAR LEFT *With his sweet, husky voice and good looks, Harry Belafonte popularised the Calypso for the white world. Alas, his screen appearances have been sporadic, and very secondary to his live concert and TV career.*

ABOVE *Trumpeter and gravel-voiced vocalist Louis Armstrong, known as Satchmo, has graced many a musical with his presence. Nobody will forget his duet with Barbra Streisand at the 'Harmonia Gardens' in* Hello, Dolly! *(20th Century-Fox, 1969).*

RIGHT *Sammy Davis Jr is a multi-talented entertainer who, sadly for filmgoers, displays his prodigious gifts more frequently on stage than on screen. A member of Frank Sinatra's 'Rat Pack', as they were known, he appeared in several films with them – including* Oceans II, Sergeants 3, *and* Robin And The 7 Hoods *(illustrated). A memorable musical appearance was his hippie revivalist preacher in* Sweet Charity *(Universal, 1969).*

FAR RIGHT *Originally one of The Supremes, the vocal group that put the Tamla Motown sound on the pop music map, the glamorous and talented Diana Ross has emerged as a major black star in her own right. Here she is as the immortal but personally doomed jazz singer, Billie Holiday, in* Lady Sings The Blues *(Paramount, 1972).*

RIGHT *Judy Garland, MGM's greatest star at the time, in* Meet Me In St. Louis *(1944). She at first rejected the role because, at 22, she did not want to revert to playing a teenage girl.*
BELOW *Judy Garland, the girl Louis B. Mayer used to call his 'monkey', advertising Max Factor face powder.*

RIGHT *The idealised MGM American family in* Meet Me In St. Louis *(1944), which included (from left to right) Joan Carroll, Harry Davenport, Mary Astor, Lucille Bremer, Leon Ames and Judy Garland.*

the golden age of musicals, *Meet Me In St Louis*, draws its visual inspiration from American turn-of-the-century paintings and design.

Louis B. Mayer loved to idealise the American family on film, the kind that Americans wished they belonged to. *Meet Me In St Louis* gently contemplates the day-to-day existence of the Smith family between the summer of 1903 and the spring of 1904. It is divided into four acts or seasons, all introduced by a photograph from an old album which then comes to life. Contained in its pages are the father and mother (Leon Ames and Mary Astor) singing 'You And I' around the piano (Arthur Freed dubbing Ames' voice); the rhythmically staged 'Trolley Song'; the haunting Halloween sequence (recently paid homage to in *ET*, 1982); and daughters Judy Garland and Margaret O'Brien in straw hats doing a cakewalk to the song 'Under The Bamboo Tree'. But, above all, Judy Garland in glowing close-ups singing 'The Boy Next Door' and 'Have Yourself A Merry Little Xmas'. The ugly duckling had suddenly grown into a swan. With her large brown eyes, high cheek-bones, and long tresses of auburn hair, she is filmed with love, the love of her future husband. During the shooting, Judy's relationship with her director was becoming warmer, soon they were living together.

Vincente Minnelli also cast a loving eye on period detail, getting authenticity from the costumes (Irene Sharaff) and set designs, all bathed in George Folsey's mellow photography. In his first colour film, Minnelli even got away with filming Garland in a deep red velvet dress beside red-haired Lucille Bremer in emerald green in a red plush room full of extras in pastel shades. The Smith's home was constructed as a continuous set of rooms, and a whole street set was built at great cost. However, it proved to be a good investment because it was used by the studio for other films for years after.

Judy Garland divorced her estranged bandleader husband David Rose and married Minnelli in 1945. In *Ziegfeld Follies* (1946), her new husband allowed her to mug outrageously in a Greer Garson send-up, 'The Great Lady Has An Interview', but she looks gorgeous. In the rest of the movie, Minnelli indulges his taste for delirious decoration including a foamy finale in which Kathryn Grayson sings 'There's Beauty Everywhere' against a background of huge rocks, nymphs and mammoth bubbles. He was also responsible for Judy's three numbers in *Till The Clouds Roll By* (1946), a fanciful all-star biopic of Jerome Kern. As Judy was pregnant, the waist line of her dress in 'Who?' had to be continually altered as her condition became more noticeable. By the time 'Look For The

ABOVE *'I Remember It Well.' Director Vincente Minnelli sitting among the posters of some of his most celebrated movies.* LEFT *A besmirched and pregnant Judy Garland tactfully placed behind a sink singing 'Look For The Silver Lining' from* Till The Clouds Roll By *(1946), MGM's lavish but highly sentimentalised biopic of Jerome Kern.*

ABOVE *Serafin, the strolling player (Gene Kelly), and Manuela, the romantic senorita (Judy Garland), in a clash of temperaments from Vincente Minnelli's* The Pirate *(1948).*

Silver Lining' was shot, Minnelli had to get her to sing it hidden behind a sink piled with pots, pans and dishes.

Minnelli purposely goes 'for theatrical, stylised settings and approach in *The Pirate*, but the editing, the colour photography, and the Cole Porter songs, wittily performed by Garland and Gene Kelly, prevent it from seeming stagey. Judy literally lets her hair down in the highly-charged 'Mack The Black', and elsewhere she and Kelly romp through this tongue-in-cheek romantic musical set on a lush Caribbean island. At the end of the 'Be A Clown' number, Judy and Gene burst into genuine laughter, and Minnelli kept the cameras rolling, but the gaiety on screen masked the real-life drama off it. The Minnelli marriage was

already going through a difficult time. Judy had started pill-popping, was consistently late on the set, broke into fits of temper and attacked her co-star and husband, accusing them of conspiring against her. It was the last film on which she and Minnelli worked together. They were divorced in 1951.

After a three-year absence from the musical, Minnelli returned to win an Oscar as Best Director for *An American In Paris*. The Hollywood musical's first post-war tribute to the French capital, it was scripted by Alan Jay Lerner around over a dozen glorious Gershwin melodies. Minnelli had already filmed ambitious, lengthy ballets in *Yolanda And The Thief* and *Ziegfeld Follies*, and once again a ballet became an essential part of a Freed musical. 'Minnelli, Irene Sharaff, Saul Chaplin (music director) and I worked in close harmony' explained Gene Kelly. 'In short, we really tried to make a ballet, not just merely a dance . . . but an emotional whole, consisting of the combined arts which spell ballet.'

The Band Wagon was virtually the only Minnelli musical to use a show business background. In fact, *The Band Wagon* is the apotheosis of the 'backstage' musical. A rare musical *á clef*, it not only plays on Fred Astaire's persona and features a songwriting team (based on the writers of the screenplay, Betty Comden and Adolph Green), but contains a dig at Minnelli's own 'artiness' in the shape of Jack Buchanan's pretentious actor-director. It ends with 'The Girl Hunt Ballet', a spoof on a lurid Mickey Spillane novel,

RIGHT *Leslie Caron, the Can-Can girl, and Gene Kelly as Chocolat in a scene inspired by Toulouse-Lautrec from the 'arty' ballet in* An American In Paris *(1951).*

'*It had to be a ballet with some kind of style, and it had to be popular. As Mickey Spillane's novels were very popular, I made it a satire on those novels . . . with beautiful girls and killings and private eyes.*'

Vincente Minnelli on 'The Girl Hunt Ballet' from The Band Wagon.

LEFT *Cyd Charisse's body was more eloquent than her voice or face, but she emerged in* The Band Wagon (1953) *as a full-blown star, obliterating the memory of the pretty, pirouetting girl of earlier films.*

121

'*We had Charles Schoenbaum as cameraman. We had shot half the picture . . . and I said to Schoenbaum, 'I don't like that red shadow on the wall.' And he said, 'I can't see a red shadow at all. It's green.' It turned out this top colour cameraman was colour-blind! And the sound man at the studio, Douglas Shearer, brother of Norma, was deaf!'*

Rouben Mamoulian on the making of Summer Holiday.

ABOVE RIGHT *Michael Kidd choreographed 'The Girl Hunt Ballet' for Minnelli's* The Band Wagon *(1953) which featured two faces of Cyd Charisse, dark-haired and tough or blonde and vulnerable shown here, tantalizing private-eye Fred Astaire.*

RIGHT *In Rouben Mamoulian's musical adaptation of Eugene O'Neill's 'Ah Wilderness!',* Summer Holiday *(1942), Marilyn Maxwell is the saloon tart Belle who gets Mickey Rooney drunker and drunker, appearing to him as a more and more scarlet woman.*

LEFT *Gene Kelly is only too pleased to show Esther Williams how to handle a bat in* Take Me Out To The Ballgame *(1949), as Jules Munshin (left) and Frank Sinatra look on enviously*.

choreographed by Michael Kidd, with a cod tough private-eye narration (written by Alan Jay Lerner) delivered by Fred with such lines as 'She was scared – scared as a turkey in November' and, aptly describing Cyd Charisse, 'she came to me in sections. She had more curves than a scenic railway.' *The Band Wagon* certainly had Entertainment.

Rouben Mamoulian, the veteran director of *Love Me Tonight* (1932), one of the most delightful of 30s musicals, was asked by Arthur Freed to direct *Summer Holiday* (1947), a musical adaptation of Eugene O'Neill's family comedy, 'Ah, Wilderness!'. Mamoulian, who had shot the first three-strip Technicolor feature, *Becky Sharp* (1933), was extremely meticulous about colour. 'I wanted to capture the quality of Americana,' he explained. 'With the yellows and light greens of Grant Wood and similar painters. I didn't want any contrasting colours at all, just tints within a narrow chromatic range. If I had a yellow wall in a room, I'd make sure the costumes would be off-yellow.' Only in one scene do the pastel shades give way to brighter colours, and only for dramatic effect. Mickey Rooney, as the adolescent suffering 'growing pains' (Rooney was then 26, twice married and divorced, once to Ava Gardner), goes to a sleazy cabaret where he meets voluptuous blonde singer Marilyn Maxwell. She is wearing a pale pink dress and a little hat with a wilting feather on it. As Mickey gets drunker and drunker, her dress becomes a deeper and deeper red and her hat gets covered in thick plumes. *Summer Holiday* is aglow with nostalgia, quintessentially MGM in its orchestration and sweep, taking a range of American institutions into its carefully constructed framework.

Busby Berkeley's last film as overall director, the Technicolored baseball musical, *Take Me Out To The Ballgame* (1949) resembled the words of the finale: 'Like a great big strawberry shortcake, or a turkey on Thanksgiving Day, like a Fourth of July, or apple pie, it's strictly USA.' Actually, Berkeley was now completely out of step with the Freed Unit, and Gene Kelly and Stanley Donen (who co-write the script), directed and choreographed all the numbers. Freed was so pleased with their work on the movie, that he asked them to direct a complete film themselves. The result was *On The Town* (1949), the first of an invigorating and innovative trilogy of films directed by the duo. Advertised as 'skirts, skyscrapers and scamperings are the theme as three skittering scamps take highways and byways of the big city!', it tells of three American sailors (Gene Kelly, Frank Sinatra and Jules Munshin) on twenty-four hours leave in New York who pair off with three girls (Vera-Ellen, Betty Garrett and Ann Miller.) The 'New York, New York' number was actually filmed on location, something unheard of in those days. Among the sights the sailors

> THERE was nothing the censors could put their fingers on. The red colour, the girl in black, and the sailor in white were very sensuous. The moves were sensuous. Yet I never laid a glove on her. There was nothing the censors could say. If they did, I could have said, What? Do you have a dirty mind? But yes, it was very sensual, and the colours did it.

ABOVE *Gene Kelly on the dream ballet in* On The Town.

ABOVE *Gene Kelly, Debbie Reynolds and Donald O'Connor come splashing into view at the opening of* Singin' In The Rain, *(1952), a foretaste of the many pleasures to come.*

equipment was used in the picture. Walter Plunkett, who did the costumes, remembered the period in which the film is set. 'Because the mikes could pick up any sound and distort it terribly, we had to use special fabrics for the costumes. Beaded dresses had to be kept to minimum, as beads would clatter a lot. . . . We couldn't use taffeta because it made such a noise.' The illusionist Freed Unit created a dubbing double bluff in the picture. Silent screen star Lina Lamont (an unforgettable performance by Jean Hagen) finds her voice to be risibly squeaky for sound movies and, unknown to the public, is dubbed by Debbie Reynolds. In reality, however, Debbie's singing voice was dubbed by the uncredited Betty Royce, and Jean Hagen herself provided the speaking voice for Debbie dubbing her on screen. Nevertheless, Debbie Reynolds, in her first major role, sparkled throughout from the moment she jumps out of an enormous cake at a party and does the Charleston in a skimpy flapper's dress. She keeps up brilliantly with Gene Kelly and Donald O'Connor in the cheery matinal greeting, 'Good Morning', danced and sung around a living room, and is touching in the lyrical duet, 'You Were Meant For Me' with Kelly, who switches on coloured lights and a gentle wind machine on a sound stage to create a make-believe atmosphere. 'I learned a lot from Gene', Debbie later admitted. 'He is a perfectionist and a disciplinarian – the most exacting director I've ever worked for. . . . Every so often he would yell at me and make me cry. But it took a lot of patience for

visit is The Empire State building. They return to it later, but this time it's a Hollywood set, far more exciting and colourful than the real thing. The sextet start to sing 'We're Going On The Town' on the top of the building, continue in the elevator, and then joyously down the street.

Most of the songs in Kelly and Donen's affectionate satire on the early days of sound, *Singin' In The Rain* (1952), are by Arthur Freed and Nacio Herb Brown. Months were spent in research to get the feel of the era, and even some original camera and sound

RIGHT *An example of the innovative and high-spirited dancing to be found in Gene Kelly and Stanley Donen's* It's Always Fair Weather (1955) *with (l to r) Michael Kidd, Gene Kelly and Dan Dailey.*

him to work with someone who had never danced before.'

The final film of the Kelly–Donen trilogy was *It's Always Fair Weather* (1955), a semi-sequel to *On The Town*. It tells of three soldier buddies (Gene Kelly, Dan Dailey and Michael Kidd) who meet up ten years after the war and find they have nothing in common, until they are brought together again in adversity. Dolores Gray, as an ingratiating TV hostess, belts out 'Thanks A Lot But No Thanks' while refusing fabulous riches from wealthy chorus boys, and 'Music Is Better Than Words', stunningly garbed by Helen Rose. Comden and Green's script takes some satirical swipes at TV, the cinema's Nemesis in the 50s. However, nowadays, TV gets its revenge by lopping off half the wide-screen image. Kelly and Donen use CinemaScope inventively, particularly when the three ex-soldiers soliloquise on what they think of the others to the tune of 'The Blue Danube', on a split screen. The film ends with the valedictory, 'The Time For Parting', as the three friends are seen, in an overhead shot, going in three different directions. *It's Always Fair Weather* was virtually the last original MGM musical of merit, and Gene Kelly and Stanley

Donen went their separate ways.

Stanley Donen's first solo effort had been *Royal Wedding* (1951) whose puerile plot was forgotten among the lively numbers performed by Fred Astaire and Jane Powell (coming in after June Allyson and Judy Garland dropped out) as a brother-sister act in London for Princess Elizabeth's marriage. The film includes the song with the longest of titles. Alan Jay Lerner got the idea one day on the way to the studio, remarking 'This picture is so damn charming it's going to delicate itself to death. What it needs is a real corny vaudeville number. How's this for a title? How Could You Believe Me When I Said I Love You When You Know I've Been A Liar All My Life?' The movie ends with a triple wedding. Astaire to Sarah Churchill, Powell to aristocrat Peter Lawford, and the real royal one. *Seven Brides For Seven Brothers* (1954), ends with six couples being married at the same time. Donen makes exuberant use of the wide screen to dance across in this wide-open spaces musical (filmed on the MGM backlot). Tall baritone Howard Keel and diminutive soprano Jane Powell make a good match, despite the disparity in their heights, and all but one (Jeff Richards) of the other redheaded brothers were

ABOVE *The sweep and style of Stanley Donen's* Seven Brides For Seven Brothers *(1954), choreographed by Michael Kidd, used the wide screen to display masculine movement at its best. Here, Matt Mattox delights his siblings and the town girls with his acrobatics.*

chosen for their dancing ability. The highlight is the acrobatic barn-raising ballet, choreographed by Michael Kidd, that ends with a fight between the brothers and the city boys.

Charles Walters, like Stanley Donen, was a former Broadway dancer and choreographer. He joined MGM as dance director in 1942 and was responsible for the dances in *Meet Me In St Louis* and *Summer Holiday*. Freed gave him the chance to direct *Good News* (1947), a zestful campus musical, where he displayed his characteristic light touch and the ability to build a number on screen. Judy Garland and Mickey Rooney were originally to have starred in it, but they were busy with other projects, personal and public. Sweet, petite, husky-voiced, 30-year-old June Allyson was given the lead as a college girl and

ABOVE *A scene from the spirited college musical* Good News *(1947), with Joan McCracken and Ray MacDonald in 'Pass That Peace Pipe'.*

RIGHT AND BELOW *Musical biopics of composers were good excuses for a series of starry numbers. June Allyson contributed her charm to* Words And Music *(1948), reputedly about Rodgers and Hart, by dancing with the Blackburn twins in 'Thou Swell', and she sang the title song of* Till The Clouds Roll By *(1946) with Ray MacDonald, a dubious tribute to Jerome Kern.*

ABOVE *Unpredictable Judy Garland responded well to the debonair Fred Astaire and the sympathetic direction of Charles Walters in* Easter Parade *(1948), another period piece for Irene to demonstrate her dress-designing skills.*

LEFT *Glacially glamorous Grace Kelly in her only musical* High Society *(1956) with her 'True Love', Bing Crosby, studying her painfully.*

Englishman Peter Lawford was cast as the All-American football hero. Although Lawford could neither sing nor dance (nor act much), Walters disguised the fact in the vigorous 'Varsity Drag' finale. Curiously, the ebullient June Allyson starred in few musicals, but made notable guest appearances in *Words And Music* (1948) singing and dancing 'Thou Swell', dwarfed between the rangy Blackburn Twins, and sang the title song of *Till The Clouds Roll By* (1946) with boyish, smiling singer-dancer Ray MacDonald. (He committed suicide in 1959 aged 38).

Charles Walters directed elegant Fred Astaire in three graceful Freed-produced musicals, *Easter Parade* (1948), *The Barkleys Of Broadway* (1949) and *The Belle Of New York* (1952), and two pleasing aquatic vehicles for Esther Williams, *Easy To Love* (1953) and *Dangerous When Wet* (1953). The latter contains a dream sequence in which Esther swims underwater with Tom and Jerry while trying to avoid an octopus in a beret who gropes her with six extra hands. No-one actually gropes Grace Kelly in Walters' *High Society* (1956), her last film before going into higher society. Dressed exquisitely by Helen Rose, she sings 'True Love' with Bing Crosby on a yacht. Although it was meant as a showcase for Grace Kelly's 'Miss Frigidaire' blonde beauty, the best number is

CEDRIC GIBBONS—ART DIRECTOR

His was the look that launched a thousand hits. His was the art – always in the correct cinematic place – that, through the 30s and into the 50s, was of profound importance in affecting the way things looked and the way people lived. Gibbons was, as Ephraim Katz wrote: 'The most celebrated and possibly the most important and influential production designer in the history of American films.'

His were the concepts of those staircases plunging like some impossible cleavage into a vast room whose angularity of design was further emphasised by a brilliant white colour scheme: you were amazed that people were allowed – or supposed – to live there.

He had begun as an art director with Edison, worked for Goldwyn for a time, and ended up where he did his best and most important work and where he found due and true appreciation – with MGM.

He designed the Oscar statuette, and went on to win it eleven times for his sets; his work influenced all other designers. Married to Dolores Del Rio, their home was a vast art-deco set design of itself.

Musicals were not, at first, his primary genre, but later as they came into their own at MGM he enjoyed the magnificence of sweep he was allowed by the munificence of finance lavished upon them: from *Cabin In The Sky* (1943) to *Kismet* (1955).

TOP RIGHT *The living room of Gibbons' home – a private reflection of his style and taste, illustrating his flair for the art deco of the period.*
CENTRE RIGHT *Mr and Mrs Gibbons at home.*
RIGHT *One of the lavish, Italianate sets by Cedric Gibbons for MGM's 1936 screen version of Shakespeare's* Romeo And Juliet.

LEFT *Cedric Gibbons surveys a scale model of one of his sets. Beside it, the Academy award statuette, or Oscar, which he designed. Top inset shows Gibbons with his wife, the celebrated Mexican screen beauty, Dolores Del Rio.*

ABOVE *Judy Garland 'had lost about fifteen or twenty pounds between the two months before we had finished cutting the picture and the time she did the last number – 'Get Happy' – and looked so beautiful that everybody thought it was a stock shot.' – Joe Pasternak, producer of* Summer Stock *(1950).*

RIGHT *The poster that shows Judy in the famous 'close-up' pose from the great film that has now had 20 minutes restored to it since its butchered release in 1954.*

the duet between Crosby and Frank Sinatra. Taking refuge at a bar during a swanky affair, they lightheartedly mock the upper crust's attitude to bad news in Cole Porter's 'Well, Did You Evah?', before dancing their way back into the party.

The plot of *Summer Stock* (1950) might have been slim, but Judy Garland was definitely overweight. Walters did his utmost to make her look good, but the high spot 'Get Happy' was shot three months after completion when Judy had lost over fifteen pounds, Wearing leotards, a tuxedo jacket and a black fedora pushed down over one eye, she looks an eyeful. None of the tensions behind the scenes of this happy-go-lucky musical is revealed on screen. It was Judy's last film for MGM.

Whereas Fred Astaire and Gene Kelly seemed to glide from one film to another with the same insouciance with which they sang and danced, each picture was wrung from Judy Garland at great expense to her physical and mental state and those around her. The autobiographical elements in *A Star Is Born* (1954) are not only contained in her role as the rising Hollywood star Vicki Lester, but in her falling self-destructive alcoholic husband Norman Maine (James Mason), who drowns himself in the sea as Judy sings (without accompaniment), 'It's A New World.' *A Star Is Born* is her greatest achievement and testament. It is also the peak of director George Cukor's career, making for Warner Bros. the best non-MGM musical since *The Wizard Of Oz* in 1939. His use of lighting, colour, costumes and space, surpass all other attempts at a musical on the wide screen, often dealing with the awkward CinemaScope shape by leaving both sides of the frame almost dark in several scenes. The film-within-a-film 'Born In A Trunk' narrative production number (inserted after Cukor had left), is kissing cousin to 'The Broadway Ballet' in *Singin' In The Rain*. A whole showbiz biography unfolds within ten minutes, ending with Judy singing 'Swanee' in minstrel gear and swinging a cane, backed by a chorus. As she explains in song, 'If you knew of all the years of hopes and dreams and tears, you'll know it didn't happen overnight.' In contrast, clad only in white shirt and black tights, Judy conjures up a gigantic production number by herself in a living room in 'Somewhere There's A Someone'. Garland declares 'Now here comes a big fat close-up' and frames her face with her hands, palms outwards, as Cukor comes in to

JUDY GARLAND JAMES MASON

WARNER BROS. PRESENT

A Star is Born

NEW SONGS *including* - "THE MAN THAT GOT AWAY" · "IT'S A NEW WORLD" · "GOTTA HAVE ME GO WITH YOU" · "SOMEONE AT LAST" · "BORN IN A TRUNK"   TECHNICOLOR   CINEMASCOPE

ALSO STARRING JACK CARSON · CHARLES BICKFORD   WITH TOM NOONAN · MOSS HART · GEORGE CUKOR · SIDNEY LUFT   HAROLD ARLEN AND IRA GERSHWIN   A TRANSCONA ENTERPRISES PROD.   MUSICAL DIRECTION BY RAY HEINDORF   PRESENTED BY WARNER BROS.

LEFT *Using every-day objects around her in the living room, Judy Garland creates a parody of a huge production number while singing 'Somewhere There's A Someone' in George Cukor's* A Star Is Born *(1954).* BELOW *A poignant moment from* A Star Is Born, *as drunken James Mason interrupts his wife Judy Garland's Oscar triumph, pleading 'I need a job!'*

catch it. After a heavenly choir and 'twenty girls come up from the floor', she is 'discovered on top of the Eiffel Tower'. Then she shifts locale to China (wearing a lampshade as a Chinese hat), Africa (she gets under a leopard-skin rug), and Brazil (using oil and vinegar bottles as maracas.)

Showing the cruel dichotomy between Judy/Vicki's private and public life, she sings an upbeat number, 'Lose That Long Face' in clown's makeup, just after an emotional scene in her dressing trailer. But the most thrilling musical moments remains the passionate torch song about the end of an affair, 'The Man That Got Away', sung in a deserted nightclub in the wee small hours. Fifteen years separate 'Over The Rainbow' from this song, and the little girl's soft tremolo has become a full-throated vibrant woman's voice, encompassing all the experiences of those years. She did not have the idyllic childhood as depicted in films like *Meet Me In St Louis*, nor did any of her marriages end happily as suggested by the final shot of *In The Good Old Summertime* (1949), in which she is seen with her little daughter Liza, but she generated a joy in living at each step along the yellow brick road towards her death from an 'incautious self over-dosage of sleeping pills' on June 22, 1969.

In *A Star Is Born*, James Mason expresses what most of the audience must feel: 'You're a great singer. . . . You've got that little something extra Ellen Terry talked about. She said star quality was that little something extra.' Glamour takes many forms as we

LEFT AND ABOVE *MGM added to the gaiety of nations by producing a string of innocuous musicals with attractive and exotic studio locations. Jane Powell and Scotty Beckett were to be found amongst the bananas in* Nancy Goes To Rio *(1950), and (insert from l to r) Jimmy Durante, Peter Lawford, Esther Williams and Ricardo Montalban in* On An Island With You *(1948).*

have perceived. It could be locale, sets, gorgeous costumes, lighting, colour, grace of movement, masculine and feminine beauty, or sex appeal, but Garland's glamour lies in the indefinable star quality, 'that little something extra.'

Judy Garland was a prize graduate of the MGM Academy of Musicals, as were a glittering parade of other stars who kept the nation toe-tapping – not only in the Arthur Freed masterpieces, but in a stream of less prestigious but no less diverting musicals throughout the 40s and 50s. Wartime audiences' spirits were lifted by Kathryn Grayson singing 'The United Nations March' in *Thousands Cheer* (1943) and there were multitudes of melodies in *Music For Millions* (1944) for the classics, and *Broadway Rhythm*

(1944) for jive. 'Hollywood Mermaid' Esther Williams swam her way through over a dozen sunny, aquamarine movies such as *Bathing Beauty* (1944), forever smiling and blowing bubbles under water. *On An Island With You* (1948) and *Pagan Love Song* (1950) were set in Honolulu and Tahiti respectively, giving Esther ample opportunity to strip down to her stylish bathing suits and take the plunge. Teenage soprano Jane Powell trilled in exotic locations in *Holiday In Mexico* (1946) and *Nancy Goes To Rio* (1950), and was part of the all-star celebration of Sigmund Romberg's music in *Deep In My Heart* (1954). In 1974 and 1976, MGM celebrated itself in two dazzling anthologies named after the song that sums up what MGM musicals were all about – *That's Entertainment*.

ABOVE *Vivian Blaine (foreground left) as Miss Adelaide in* Guys And Dolls *(1955).*   RIGHT *Barbra Streisand (centre) in* Funny Girl *(1968).*

BROADWAY MELODIES

Your troubles there are out of style,
For Broadway always wears a smile.
A million lights they flicker there,
A million hearts beat quicker there.
No skies of gray
On that Great White Way.
That's the Broadway Melody.

Lyrics by Arthur Freed
first sung in
The Broadway Melody (1929)

'Please Don't Monkey With Broadway' sang Fred Astaire and George Murphy in *Broadway Melody Of 1940*, a caveat that Hollywood could well have applied to itself. Tinsel Town has always raised its glossy top hat in recognition of Broadway glitter by glamorising the famous Manhattan avenue. In 1929 alone, film studios turned out *The Broadway Melody*, *Lord Byron Of Broadway*, *Broadway*, *Broadway Babies*, *Broadway Scandals* and *Gold Diggers Of Broadway*, holding out a prospect of gaiety and enchantment to enthralled filmgoers. For over two decades, studios lavished fortunes on celluloid transplants from Broadway in the hope of repeating their success, but although many song-and-dance movies drew their inspiration from Broadway, they bore little resemblance to the stage originals. When the title in bright lights outside a cinema was the same as that of a Broadway show, audiences did not expect to see anything similar. Either the plot was completely changed, or few of the songs of the original remained. Stage and screen musicals continued to be separate entities providing their own particular definitions of glamour. East coast was east and west coast was west and the twain seldom met. However, when new ground was broken by Rodgers and Hammerstein's 'Oklahoma!' of 1943, with its songs integrated into the action, it was not so easy for film studios to 'monkey with Broadway', and in the fifties moviegoers began to demand that a film adaptation be as close to its source as possible. So from *Annie Get Your Gun* (1950) to *Annie* (1982), film makers have tackled the problem of how to transport a Broadway show to

'*Perhaps the most overpraised dance film yet made, it tried so hard to generate art from the violence of street warfare that it became bombastic kitsch.*'

Ballet critic Arlene Croce on West Side Story

RIGHT *The miracle that is the musical had been able to make The Sharks, a tough street gang, perform complicated ballet steps through the streets of New York in* West Side Story *(United Artists 1961).*

RIGHT *Shirley MacLaine as a taxi-dancer giving her considerable all in the 'If They Could See Me Now' number from Bob Fosse's gaudy* Sweet Charity *(Universal 1969).*

Hollywood without dissipating its individual flavour on the long journey from the boards to celluloid.

Film is a more realistic medium than theatre, and, since the fifties attempts have continually been made to circumvent or break down the inherent naturalism imposed by the camera, to lessen the artificiality of people expressing their emotions through song and dance. Joseph Mankiewicz's lively and lavish *Guys And Dolls* (1955) cannily used a stylised Times Square setting with billboards, neon lights and painted cycloramas in which to place Damon Runyon's colourful street characters, extracted from his fairy tales of New York. On the other hand, *West Side Story* (1961) opens with a helicopter view of Manhattan shot straight down and zooming in on the finger-snapping youth gang of Jets. Because it was filmed on location on West 64th Street, it emphasized rather than diminished the unreality of the gang – dancing down the streets to Jerome Robbins' balletic steps only seemed admissable later when the film resorted to studio sets. Robbins explained the difficulties. 'Dancing is not realistic, but much of the action of *West Side Story* is extremely realistic – as realistic as sudden death – with two rival gangs battling for their existence. The problem, then, was to weld the two, reality and

FAR LEFT AND LEFT *One of the most illustrious of Broadway musicals,* Oklahoma! *(20th Century-Fox 1955), was brought to the wide Todd-AO screen with much of its sweep intact. Sweet Shirley Jones song 'Many A New Day' to a chorus of corseted girls in one scene, and Agnes De Mille recreated her stage choreography for the 'Out Of My Dreams' ballet in the other.*

dramatic unreality.' In contrast, Bob Fosse told 'New York Magazine', 'Today I get very antsy watching musicals in which people are singing as they walk down the street or hang out the laundry. In fact, I think it looks a little silly. You can do it on stage. The theatre has its own personality – it conveys a removed reality. The movies bring that reality closer.' Fosse's first musical, *Sweet Charity* (1969), failed because of an over-reliance on stage structure, over-emphatic direction and an over-strident central performance from Shirley MacLaine's golden-hearted hooker. For *Cabaret* (1972), he wisely jettisoned most of the stage musical, refusing to 'open out' the numbers, and keeping the sleazy nightclub at the centre of the film.

klahoma! (1955) – shot on location in Arizona(!) for the wide open spaces of the Todd-AO screen – merely reiterated the spirit of the great outdoors as generated by the words and music of Oscar Hammerstein II and Richard Rodgers in songs like 'Oh, What A Beautiful Morning!', 'The Surrey With The Fringe On Top', and the rousing title song. None of the numbers except 'Kansas City', filmed at a railway depot and on top of a train, extended very far beyond their stage conception. George Cukor's *My Fair Lady* (1964) tended towards the photographed play, adding nothing to the theatrical experience. The 'Ascot Gavotte' was treated in the same unrealistic manner as on stage, but with many more female extras to parade Cecil Beaton's wittily chic adaptations of Edwardian fashions.

Joshua Logan, in *South Pacific* (1958), had so little confidence that audiences would accept people singing extemporaneously in natural settings – an island paradise filmed in Fiji and Hawaii – that he flooded the screen with colour filters hoping to match the moods of the songs, but only succeeding in turning the characters from blue, to green, to orange and to yellow. The technique lends mystery to 'Bali Ha'i', 'dat special islan'' shrouded in mists, but is risible when Mitzi Gaynor sings 'when the sky is a bright canary yellow' and then proceeds to go through various stages of jaundice.

Technicolor added another dimension to the third screen version of *Show Boat* (1951) with the pearly white paddle-steamer ploughing up a limpid Mississippi (actually the jungle lake built for the Tarzan pictures), and *The Sound Of Music* (1965) was

BELOW *Sad Mitzi Gaynor driving home through an appropriately blue landscape in Joshua Logan's* South Pacific *(20th Century-Fox 1958), a film misguidedly flooded with colour filters.*

enhanced by the picture-postcard Tyrolean hills 'alive with music' among which it seemed perfectly normal to break into song. *The Pajama Game* (1957) and *Damn Yankees* (1958), both co-directed by Stanley Donen and George Abbott, remained true to the stage originals while liberating much of the action by using the cinema's ability to bring about greater visual-aural harmony with creative editing. Oddly, it is the Broadway shows about the theatre like *Kiss Me Kate* (1953), *Gypsy* (1962) and *Funny Girl* (1968) that have transferred best to the screen, where the camera relishes the limited but larger-than-life arena of greasepaint, masks and illusions.

As witnessed in Gene Kelly's *Hello, Dolly!* (1969), the large screen seems to demand more elaborate choreography than the stage. Fox spent $2 million alone on a recreation of early New York City filled with a passing parade of thousands of brightly costumed extras. In the theatre it was just plausible that a mature, widowed marriage-broker would be welcomed with such overwhelming enthusiasm, after ten years' absence, by the whole staff of the luxurious Harmonia Gardens restaurant, but the film's inflated title number, choreographed by Michael Kidd, submerges any reality. The multitude of scarlet-coated waiters are, in fact, not greeting Dolly Levi but

ABOVE *Langorously lovely Ava Gardner, as the mulatto, Julie Laverne in* Show Boat *(MGM 1951), rendering the impassioned 'Bill' with an enraptured Fuzzy Knight at the piano.*

RIGHT *The spectacular 'Before The Parade Passes By' number from* Hello, Dolly! *(20th Century-Fox 1969), the film in which director Gene Kelly caught some of the old time MGM musical magic.*

LEFT *Gene Kelly (on the right), one of the most creative forces in the heyday of the film musical of the 50s, seen here directing a moment from the Harmonia Gardens restaurant scene in* Hello, Dolly! *(20th Century-Fox 1969).*

BELOW *Two original production designs, one (above) for the scarlet-coated waiters' dance, and the other for Dolly's entrance down the staircase, both set in the extraordinarily extravagant Harmonia Gardens restaurant in* Hello, Dolly! *(20th Century-Fox 1969).*

26-year-old Barbra Streisand, somehow transported back to turn-of-the-century New York where she also happens to meet Louis Armstrong in the same red plush café.

Movies may have more *dramatis personae*, more sets, more costumes, bigger orchestrations and bigger stars than the theatre, but the performances have to be toned down for the camera. The special magic that communicates itself across the footlights from such stage luminaries as Ethel Merman, Mary Martin, Carol Channing and Gwen Verdon, has barely flickered on the screen. Film ungallantly exposes the physical inadequacies of an actor or actress. Merman, who had devoured everything and everybody around her in *Call Me Madam* (1953), was not requested to repeat her tremendous stage performance in the film of *Gypsy*. Rosalind Russell as the monstrous stage mother, being a more attractive woman and a wonderful movie actress, was able to gain more sympathy for the character, while Mitzi Gaynor in *South Pacific* and Julie Andrews in *The Sound Of Music* radiated a youthfulness that the middle-aged Mary Martin, the creator of the roles, could not have got away with. However, Barbra Streisand and Liza Minnelli have maintained their magnetism on both stage and screen, displacing conventional aesthetics of feminine beauty on film.

Musicals are the most escapist of all film genres,

139

RIGHT *Two 'straight' performers who carried their songs perfectly in their only screen musical Guys And Dolls (Goldwyn 1955) – Jean Simmons as Sarah Brown the Salvation Army lass, and Marlon Brando as Sky Masterson the gambler, drinking 'Bacardi milk shakes' at a Havana nightspot.*

BELOW *Saul Bass's distinctive and angular designs for posters and credit titles generally gave the films of director Otto Preminger, such as Porgy And Bess, a boost.*

RIGHT *The beauty of Dorothy Dandridge is set against the slums of Catfish Row as she sings (with Adele Addison's voice), 'I Loves You, Porgy' from producer Samuel Goldwyn's last film, Porgy And Bess (Columbia 1959).*

antidotes to solemnity. Entertainment and glamour have never been associated with enlightenment. Little has been allowed to interfere with the hackneyed boy-meets-girl and rags-to-riches plots. Their message is generally 'There's no business *but* show business.' They have never concerned themselves inordinately with serious issues. Stage musicals have been slightly bolder in the treatment of touchy subjects, but when they reach the screen the beast has been tamed by beauty. John O'Hara's sleazy nocturnal world and Lorenz Hart's lyrics were sanitised in Columbia's *Pal Joey* (1957) and the 'gilt-edged heel' hoofer was changed into a caddish but likeable singer for Frank Sinatra, flanked by Rita Hayworth, in her last bloom, and cool ash-blonde Kim Novak.

All the blacks of Catfish Row, a deprived area of Charleston, South Carolina in 1912 in Otto Preminger's ponderous *Porgy And Bess* (1959) speak with cultivated accents, and both Sidney Poitier as the crippled beggar Porgy and Dorothy Dandridge as Bess, have glossy Hollywood good looks out of keeping with Gershwin's great folk opera. Though the members of the street gangs in *West Side Story* are meant to be in their teens, the ages of the rather clean-cut dancers ranged from 22 to 30. Irene Sharaff won an Oscar for her costume designs for these slum denizens. At great expense, the boys' blue jeans were dyed, re-dyed and 'distressed' to appear worn, and specially woven with elastic thread to allow for violent movement. Yet the galvanic dances, the music of Leonard Bernstein, and Stephen Sondheim's lyrics at least offered elements of social consciousness even if seen in radical chic show business terms.

South Pacific doesn't evade the issue of racial prejudice but, because everybody, including the Polynesians, keeps changing colour, the problem is easily resolved. In *Finian's Rainbow* (1968) there is a song called 'When The Idle Poor Become The Idle Rich' and a bigoted senator from the state of Missitucky is changed into a black man, but any social message in Fred Astaire's last musical, is drowned in indigestible Irish whimsy.

Workers demands for a seven-and-a-half cent pay rise at a pyjama factory is the unlikely subject of *The Pajama Game*, a bouncy and infectious musical. The workers, at their 'Once A Year Day' picnic, cavort in multi-coloured costumes on a green river bank in Bob Fosse's robust choreography and, of course, the head of the workers' grievance committee (delicious Doris Day) falls in love with the foreman (John Raitt). In *Annie* (1982), a cute, little carrot-topped, curly-haired

ABOVE *Poverty, pimping, prostitution and pilfering were sanitized and set to music in Carol Reed's popular Oscar-winning* Oliver! *(Columbia 1968). Three Dickensian faces – Mark Lester (left) in the title role asking for more, Shani Wallis (centre) as Nancy, and Ron Moody as Fagin.*

LEFT *Aileen Quinn, the carrot-topped moppet, in the process of livening up the Depression with her piping voice in John Huston's orphan-and-dog musical* Annie *(Columbia 1982).*

141

orphan – like the Shirley Temple of yesteryear – melts the hard heard of a plutocrat and influences President Roosevelt's policy during the Depression. The film, and the Depression presumably, ends abruptly with fireworks and a circus. The excellent *Cabaret* almost succeeds in eliminating the suspicion that a slick musical is not the best vehicle to comment on the rise of Nazism.

The first film adaptations from Broadway shows, like *The Desert Song* (1929) and *Rio Rita* (1929), suffered from bad sound and static camera set-ups. The latter was structured like a two-act musical with the second half shot entirely in colour. Warners brought Broadway's most glowing star, Marilyn Miller, to Hollywood to recreate her most famous roles in Jerome Kern's *Sally* (1929) and *Sunny* (1930). (Miller, who only made three films, died of food poisoning in 1936.) Cole Porter's shipboard romance *Anything Goes* (1936) survived with few of the original songs intact, and the lyrics of 'You're The Top', sung by Bing Crosby and Ethel Merman, were completely revised. In 1943, Lucille Ball's bright red hair was a feature in two Technicolored MGM Broadway transfers, George Abbott's *Best Foot Forward* and Cole Porter's *Du Barry Was A Lady*, both of which changed or discarded everything that had made the shows hits on stage.

Kurt Weill's musicals also suffered from Holly-

wood's cavalier treatment of his material. Little of his score remained in Paramount's psychological musical, *Lady In The Dark* (1944). The gorgeous Technicolor intensified the importance of the extraordinary costumes designed by Mitchell Leisen (the film's director), Raoul Pene Du Bois and Edith Head. Ginger Rogers as a fashion editor with her hair up, has Freudian dreams with her hair down. During a dream sequence set in a fashion-styled circus, she discards her wide $35,000 mink skirt, to reveal another one

ABOVE *John Boles and Bebe Daniels in* Rio Rita *(RKO 1929), the second all-talkie adaptation of a Broadway musical. The latter half was shot entirely in colour.*

OPPOSITE *Chorus girls at the sleazy Kit Kat Club presenting the garish floor-show in Bob Fosse's* Cabaret *(Allied Artists 1972), set in the seedy glamour of 30s Berlin.*
LEFT *Tambourines and castanets provided the music in this Moorish scene from* The Desert Song *(Warner Bros. 1929), the first all-talking, all-dancing transplant from Broadway.*

RIGHT *Ginger Rogers in one of the fabulous gowns designed for her in* Lady In The Dark *(Paramount 1944), an extravagant escape from the frugality of the war years.*

glistening with silver and gold sequins. She also wears a wedding gown, distorted in her dream to gigantic proportions. All this intimates that a woman's place is in a wedding dress, and that her obsession with clothes disguises her fear of the naked body ie sex. Much of it is triggered off when Rogers, in a severely tailored suit, meets handsome film star Jon Hall. 'I was so afraid I'd run into a glamour girl tonight,' he says relieved. 'I'm up to my hips in glamour most of the time.'

In 1950, with the MGM – Arthur Freed production of *Annie Get Your Gun*, Hollywood achieved the first faithful film adaptation of a Broadway smash. Betty Hutton, restraining some of her excesses, was convincing as Annie Oakley, the sharpshooter who is forced to conclude that 'You Can't Get A Man With A Gun', and the tall, powerfully built baritone, Howard Keel, making his Hollywood debut, was dubbed 'A Gable who sings.' Director George Sidney captured the swirl and colour of a Wild West Show, taking full

HAYS CODE: Self-regulatory Censorship

Will H. Hays was, in 1922, made head – by the major Hollywood Studios – of the new Motion Picture Producers and Distributors of America (MPPDA) as a way to alter the Hollywood image which had been much dented by various scandals. In 1930 the MPPDA, by then known as the Hays Office, created the Motion Picture Producers Code, which became known as the Hays Code. It was described as a self-regulating charter. The Hays administration ended in 1945, but the Code lingered on until 1966. In 1968 a rating system – tagging a film for old or young – came into being; it had been used before, of course, but was now a much more solid apparatus.

It was, as cynics might have prophesied, inevitable that the Hays Production Code would conflict with musicals at some time or another. The Code had a whole apparatus for determining what was or was not to be put on screen in the American cinema – and that inevitable collision was obvious because musicals, after all, were to do with a remarkably light-hearted view of human relationships. The musical *I'm No Angel* (1933) may well have helped to establish the Code in the first place, with Mae West's flaunting of sexuality as though to the Victorian vaudeville born, and its innuendoes which were not just doubled but quadrupled.

Then again, in 1934, excisions were forced upon Miss West's *Belle Of The Nineties*, although the extravagant nature of her temperament meant that the message was amply conveyed in those broad hips and that swellegant bosom – 'It's better to be looked over than overlooked.'

While Mae's disregards had gone West, the Hays Office was more effective with others – changing the title of 'The Gay Divorce', for instance, to *The Gay Divorcee* (1934) on the grounds that no divorce could ever be gay in the happy sense of the word. (Today's meaning of 'gay' would promote even more problems).

While Busby Berkeley musicals seemed to escape the Hays wrath, despite some highly suggestive dance numbers and risqué dialogue, the influence of Hays pursued others, persisting into the 1940s when the Sheik Of Araby dance number in *Tin Pan Alley* (1940) was cut because it showed too much flesh.

'It was always a difficult job,' wrote Will Hays. The difficulty was, of course, in interpretation. For one girl's dance number might well be another man's sexual invitation. It all depended what kind of mind you had.

The British, by comparison, have no film censorship established by statute, since local authorities were held responsible at first. But in 1912 the British Board of Film Censors (BBFC) was set up. Films are submitted voluntarily to the BBFC and because there is no formal code the Board can act as it thinks best in judgements.

Hays, for the record, was a lawyer and US Post Master General in President Harding's cabinet. The administration in which he wielded so much power was ended in 1945, but the code stood as the American reaction to the immorality until 1966 even though the principle had long since been violated.

'THOU SHALT NOT'
1 LAW DEFEATED
2 INSIDE OF THIGH
3 LACE LINGERIE
4 DEAD MAN
5 NARCOTICS
6 DRINKING
7 EXPOSED BOSOM
8 GAMBLING
9 POINTING GUN
10 TOMMY GUN

ABOVE *Entitled 'How To Shoot The Stars', this famous poster designed by Whitey Schafer, eloquently sums up (and parodies) Hollywood's own sacred tablet of commandments as defined by the almighty Will Hays and his censorship code. The musical frequently found a way round the restrictions imposed on less glamorous material.*

RIGHT *Frenetic Betty Hutton claiming that 'I'm An Indian, Too' much to the satisfaction of J. Carrol Naish as Chief Sitting Bull in a Robert Alton production number from* Annie Get Your Gun *(MGM 1950).*

BELOW *Keenan Wynn and James Whitmore (left) witness the taming of shrewish Kathryn Grayson by macho Howard Keel in Cole Porter's witty musical-within-a-musical,* Kiss Me Kate *(MGM 1953).*

advantage of the camera in the outdoor sequences. The finale, a parade of hundreds of horses forming patterns, justified the accompanying lusty rendering of 'There's No Business Like Show Business.'

George Sidney also directed Cole Porter's witty *Kiss Me Kate* (1953), giving Howard Keel, Kathryn Grayson and Ann Miller their most rewarding roles. 'The Hollywood Reporter' wrote that MGM has 'blended wonderful, colourful sets into optical orgies, using them as backgrounds for gay musical numbers.' Two of them were Hermes Pan's zesty, 'From This Moment On' danced by Miller, Tommy Rall, Bobby Van, Bob Fosse, Carol Haney and Jeannie Coyne (Gene Kelly's second wife), and Ann Miller's comedic 'Always True To You In My Fashion.'

True to the Broadway originals in his fashion, Vincente Minnelli tackled the awkward dimensions of the CinemaScope screen with *Brigadoon* (1954) and *Kismet* (1955), almost confirming Sam Goldwyn's maxim that 'a wide screen makes a bad film twice as bad.' *Brigadoon* still casts a certain spell despite the feyness and the painted scenery simulating the romantic Scottish Highlands where Gene Kelly and Van Johnson come across an enchanted village that emerges only once a century from the mists. Towards the end, Minnelli creates a violent contrast between a bustling Manhattan containing Kelly's fiancee, and the picturesque Scottish village and the lovely girl (Cyd Charisse) with whom he had danced through the 'Heather On The Hill.' Amidst the Oriental kitsch and pantomimic prancings of *Kismet* are the songs, with words set to the music of Alexander Borodin (a 'borrowed din' as some wit unfairly commented), put over with gusto by Howard Keel and Dolores Gray, and with sweetness by Ann Blyth and Vic Damone, making it a Turkish Delight of a musical.

In the mid-50s, 20th Century-Fox began to take over from MGM as the studio of musicals, transposing five of Rodgers and Hammerstein's oeuvre to the Todd-AO screen, the 70mm process with its six-track stereophonic sound. Although technically advanced, these protracted, reverent, loud and mushy movies were retreats from the contemporary world and contemporary cinema – and vastly popular. The first, *Oklahoma!* (1955), retained some of its folksy, fresh-air quality with the help of Oliver Smith's production design and Orry-Kelly's costumes of calico, denim, and crocheted lace, giving the movie an American Primitive look. Shirley Jones, in her first film, is a pretty picture of salubrity and Gordon MacRae the good-looking hero who rescues her from the clutches of sinister, unshaven hired hand Rod

ABOVE *American tourist Gene Kelly romancing Scots lass Cyd Charisse in dance in Vincente Minnelli's Highland fantasy,* Brigadoon *(MGM 1954), filmed in a sound stage near the Hollywood Hills rather than the hills of Scotland.*
LEFT *Sebastian Cabot (left) as the Wazir, Mike Mazurki (centre) and Howard Keel as Haaj the beggar-poet among the gilt of Vincente Minnelli's 'Turkitsch' musical* Kismet *(MGM 1955).*

RIGHT *Cameron Mitchell (centre with concertina), a New England setting, 'A Real Nice Clambake', a Rodgers and Hammerstein musical – Carousel (20th Century-Fox 1956).*

BELOW *A colourful clash of characters and culture between Yul Brynner as King Somdetch P'hra Paaremndr Maha Mongkut and English governess Deborah Kerr as Anna Leonowens, with Rita Moreno as the King's eldest daughter Tuptim caught in the middle, in* The King And I *(20th Century-Fox 1956).*

Steiger, Successfully cast against type was Gloria Grahame as the coquettish, red-haired Ado Annie.

Gordon MacRae and Shirley Jones were paired again in *Carousel* (1956), set in the New England of the 1870s and shot on location, principally at Boothbay Harbor, Maine. Frank Sinatra was first cast as the roguish, fairground barker Billy Bigelow, but he walked out after a few days filming. As the film was to be shot in both 55mm and 33mm CinemaScope, the cast was required to perform each scene twice and Sinatra didn't wish to make two movies for the price of one. (It turned out that no dual filming was necessary.) The film opens with Billy in a tinkling glassy-starred heaven from where he looks back on his curtailed life. Some of the movie's treacle is washed away by the 'Soliloquy', sung by MacRae against the pounding of waves on rocks, and the rollicking 'June Is Bustin' Out All Over' with dancers jumping off roofs.

The lustrous-domed Yul Brynner as the King of Siam, in a radiant royal raiment of Thai silks embroidered with gold and jewels, sturdy bare feet apart, dominated *The King And I* (1956) as powerfully as he did his league of wives and children. It is a balletic performance, though he dances but once in the 'Shall We Dance?' polka, a noble savage embracing the embodiment of Victorian values in the corseted, wide-hooped shape of Deborah Kerr. The contrast between her confined lady-like manner and his unrestrained masculine movements mirrors the cultural and character clash. Kerr found the Irene Sharaff gowns heavy and painful to move around in, as the hoops were made of metal. She had to put foam rubber on her hips to prevent injury. As cumbersome was Walter Lang's direction, but cultural convergence was lightly and amusingly portrayed in Jerome Robbins' 'The Small House Of Uncle Thomas' ballet, in which an American tale is told in traditional Thai terms.

I n contrast to the opulence and sentimentality of the Rodgers and Hammerstein blockbusters, Broadway also followed a more brash, razzle-dazzle, gutsy tradition of music and glamour. *Damn Yankees* (1958) was a diabolical musical, only in the sense of being another version of the Faust legend. Gwen Verdon repeated her stage role as the Devil's handmaiden given the job of vamping baseball player Tab Hunter. The flame-haired Verdon does a 'straight seduction job' on the handsome, crew-cutted sportsman. With a phony Spanish accent and a rose between her teeth, she strips down to black lace underwear.

However, for stylish seduction, pezazz and dynamism, there is nothing to touch *Gypsy* (1962), arguably the best ever screen transfer of a Broadway musical.

Mervyn LeRoy, the director, aided by the Technicolor camerawork of Harry Stradling and the art direction of John Beckman, found filmic equivalents for the theatrical atmosphere of the play. The film sweeps from the seedy glamour of the vaudeville stage onto which Rosalind Russell's Mama Rose shoves her daughters June (Ann Jilliann) and Louise (Natalie Wood), to the triumph of Louise, renamed Gypsy Rose Lee, as the supreme stripper of her day in 'classy'

ABOVE *Ray Walston as the Devil, known as Mr Applegate, and a subdued Gwen Verdon as his beautiful 172-year-old assistant in* Damn Yankees *(Warner Bros. 1958).*

LEFT *Juliet Prowse at the centre of the riotous dance finale of* Can-Can *(20th Century-Fox 1960), a grotesque attempt to capture the Paris of Auguste Renoir and Lautrec.*

burlesque houses. In a sensitive portrayal of the famous stripper, Natalie Wood blossomed from the insecure teenager forced to wear boy's clothes for her mother's act, into a self-confident woman, beautified by fame. Almost every number is a celebration of show business ambition, the inextricably linked yearning for love and renown, such as the get-up-and-go 'Some People', the determinedly optimistic 'Everything's Coming Up Roses' sung in the bluish melancholy of a railway station as Rose transfers her ambitions from one daughter to another, and in a back alley a young hoofer (Paul Wallace), singing 'All I Need Is The Girl', demonstrates the routine with which he hopes to conquer Broadway. He is joined by Natalie Wood with whom he reaches an orgiastic climax with the words, 'Again, Again, Again.' This is echoed by Russell in 'Rose's Turn' where on an empty stage with her name emblazoned in lights behind her, she does a striptease in mime which effectively also bares her soul, ending with the egotistical cry, 'For Me, For Me, For Me.'

Gypsy cost Warner Bros. $3 million. Jack Warner paid $5 million for the screen rights alone of *My Fair Lady* (1964), making it one of the most expensive musicals in history. As with *Gigi* (1958), the production design and costumes of Cecil Beaton were essential components of its success. Beaton claimed that theatre should 'shower the spectator with illusions not to be found at home', and he showered the spectators of the film with a multitude of resplendent dresses and meticulously researched sets. Upholstery and carpets were woven to order, wallpaper was specially printed in England to a William Morris design, and antique shops in California were combed for the correct *objets d'arts*, old gramophones, washstands, door knobs and even a cigar box for Professor Higgins' study. Audrey Hepburn as Eliza Doolittle proved an exquisite model for a ball-gown and a white lace Ascot dress with striped ribbons and crowned with an immense hat. However, she clearly needed a real-life Professor Higgins to teach her in

‛I grabbed as much as I could from the stage, and that's also a trick: to take something from the stage and not make it stodgy, to make it flow. But this scene (the Ascot Gavotte) had an artificial style . . . like a ballet'

George Cukor, director of My Fair Lady.

LEFT *Audrey Hepburn as Eliza Doolittle in* My Fair Lady *(Warner Bros. 1964) wearing the famous Edwardian black-and-white Ascot ensemble created by Cecil Beaton in the grand tradition of motion picture costume design.*

151

ABOVE *The hills are alive with the singing voices of Julie Andrews and the seven Von Trapp children in* The Sound Of Music *(20th Century-Fox 1965), filmed on location in Austria in magnificent Todd-AO and De Luxe Color.*

RIGHT *'Uneasy lies the head that wears the crown'. Richard Harris as King Arthur making a strenuous effort to sing in* Camelot *(Warner Bros. 1967), the $15 million musical with exceptional costumes made from coarse linen and raw silk and designed by John Truscott.*

reverse how to be convincing as a cockney gutter-snipe.

Julie Andrews, who had been ousted by Hepburn for the Eliza role, won an Oscar for her first film, *Mary Poppins*, in the same year, and got her over-sweet revenge by reaching the peak of stardom in *The Sound Of Music* (1965). Andrews is first discovered joyously singing the title song at the top of her voice (and an Austrian Alp), having taken the Mother Abbess's exhortation to 'Climb Every Mountain' literally. This unabashedly old-fashioned, *gemütlich* and mawkish musical containing seven lovable children, their handsome and wealthy widower father, a rookery of nuns and a fresh-faced, liberty-loving singing governess, set against superb Tyrolean scenery, is placed in the top ten box-office movies of all time.

Brooklyn-born Barbra Streisand also won the Best Actress Oscar for her film debut as comedienne-singer Fanny Brice in *Funny Girl* (1968). The sixties was a period of alternative life-styles and alternative looks. Yet the movie is full of self-conscious references to Streisand's unclassical features, the large nose and mouth, the eyes a little too close together. Her mother

❛The real, real reason I like to be in movies is because it's an easy place to have hems done. There's always a seamstress on the set. And if you break a chair, they can fix it – they have people who can do anything. Chair people, hem people.❜

Barbra Streisand

LEFT *'I'm The Greatest Star'* *sings Barbra Streisand in* Funny Girl *(Columbia 1968), forcing audiences to reassess their preconceived notions of beauty.*

RIGHT *Although miscast, Barbra Streisand almost merits the excessively enthusiastic welcome she receives by the staff of the Harmonia Gardens restaurant in the ever-repeated title number from* Hello, Dolly! *(20th Century-Fox 1969).*
BELOW *Under hypnosis, Brooklynese Barbra Streisand finds herself at an orphanage in 18th century England, but is soon transformed into a beauty in Vincente Minnelli's* On A Clear Day You Can See Forever *(Paramount 1970).*

deplores the fact that 'If A Girl Isn't Pretty', she hasn't much chance in show business, Streisand sings 'His Love Makes Me Beautiful', and makes a crack at herself in a wedding scene with 'the groom was prettier than the bride.' But when she sings in her throbbing, soaring voice, 'I'm The Greatest Star' with conviction, nobody would argue with her.

The ribbing of Barbra Streisand's appearance diminished from film to film as she became accepted as a genuinely glamorous superstar. Irene Sharaff dressed her for *Hello, Dolly!* (1969), her shimmering gold gown and hat of yellow and orange ostrich feathers standing out against the red and black in the title number, and Cecil Beaton gave her new elegance in *On A Clear Day You Can See Forever* (1970), Beaton's last film and Vincente Minnelli's penultimate one. Barbra is credible as both Daisy Gamble from Brooklyn and an 18th century beauty called Melinda Wainwhistle whom she becomes under hypnosis. Among Beaton's Regency costumes is a ball gown of white silk embroidered with silver beads and pearls worn by Streisand as if she had never heard of Brooklyn. Shot among the Chinoiserie of the Royal

Pavilion in Brighton, the film is directed with Minnelli's abiding visual distinction.

It is inconceivable that the progeny of Vincente Minnelli and Judy Garland would not have entered show business. Liza Minnelli has all the star quality inherited from her mother, but she is too close not to suffer by comparison. Liza's urgent delivery, intensity, warm vibrato and the over-whelming desire to put herself across recall Judy Garland. But she is too self-aware to be truly tragic, her verve and her humour always lurking close to the surface of her pathos. In *Cabaret* (1972), Liza's large puppy's eyes, clown's mouth and awkward stance make her look like Louise Brooks seen through a distorting mirror. Liza's brash, tough, kookie personality was perfectly suited to the role of Sally Bowles, American nightclub singer at the Kit Kat Club in Berlin in the last years of the Weimar Republic. No matter that she is too good a singer to be found in such a seamy club, Bob Fosse's movie captures the essence of Berlin in the early thirties, filtered through the Expressionist paintings of the

ABOVE *(left to right) Antonia Ellis, Georgina Hale, Caryl Little and Sally Bryant in an orgy of ogling from Ken Russell's* The Boy Friend *(MGM 1971), an overblown screen version of a modestly likeable stage musical.*

LEFT *Liza Minnelli's bravura singing and acting as Sally Bowles brought Broadway showbiz oomph to Berlin in the 30s, and plenty of heart to Bob Fosse's flashy* Cabaret *(Allied Artists 1972).*

ABOVE *Epicene Master of Ceremonies Joel Grey (recreating his stage role) and the Kit Cat Girls, representing decadence in* Cabaret *(Allied Artists 1972).*

RIGHT *Centre stage of a rock light show is Carl Anderson as Judas, one of the most demanding roles in the Andrew Lloyd-Webber/ Tim Rice musical* Jesus Christ Superstar *(Universal 1973), filmed on location in Israel.*

156

period, the books of Christopher Isherwood, and the Brecht-Weill operas. The cabaret is a metaphor, and the epicene emcee (Joel Gray) the face of decadence. The songs of John Kander and Fred Ebb offer a mixture of pastiche and Broadway numbers like the title song, put over by Liza Minnelli with all the anachronistic ardour of a star of the 70s. 'Life is a cabaret', she sings and the musical endorses this.

'The loveliest corpse I've ever seen', a lyric from *Cabaret*, might be an appropriate description of the film musical. Unfortunately, this most glamorous of film genres is an endangered species. The musical conceived especially for the screen is virtually extinct, and even Broadway transfers have become few and far between. *A Little Night Music* (1977) turned a lightly waltzing chamber musical into a clod-hopping attempt to recapture the opulence of turn-of-the-century Viennese operetta; *Grease* (1978), the most popular musical in motion picture history, was bubble gum for the ears and eyes with a 50s flavouring; and while *Hair* (1979) offered vigorous dancing through the streets and parks of New York, its Flower Power paraphernalia had already withered. Barbra Streisand, Liza Minnelli, John Travolta and Bette Midler are the few who have the presence that makes great song-and-dance stars, but the dearth of musicals in the last decade has given them scant opportunity to display it. It is not enough to wallow in the myriads of musicals of the past with their parade of glittering

LEFT *Glamour galore is always in evidence when Elizabeth Taylor is around, but she and director Harold Prince managed to destroy the indestructible songs of Stephen Sondheim in* A Little Night Music *(1977).*

stars. Yet, hope still comes from Broadway, where musicals fill the majority of theatres. As long as there is someone there to shout, as in *Gypsy*, 'Curtain up, light the lights, You have nothing to hit but the heights,' someone in Hollywood is going to want to satisfy the human craving for the nostalgia, escapism and romance which finds its fullest expression in the glamour of the screen musical.

LEFT *Theadora Van Runkle's close-fitting costumes for blonde and bosomy Dolly Parton (centre), and other members of* The Best Little Whorehouse In Texas *(Universal 1982), left little to the imagination.*

INDEX

Page numbers in *italic's* refer to illustrations, figures in parentheses refer to mentions on the page.

A

Abbott, George 138, 143
Adrian 19, 21, 22, 23, 28, 29, 35, 38, 59, 83, 111
Affairs Of Dobie Gillis, The 79
Alexander's Ragtime Band 87
All About Eve 91
All That Jazz 80
Allen, Debbie *80*
Allen, Gene 30
Allen, Gracie 64
Allyson, June 125, 126
Alton, Robert 146
Ameche, Don 88, 90
American In Paris, An 12, 30, 74, 76, 110, 115, 120
Ames, Leon *118*, 119
Anchors Aweigh 28, 74
And The Angels Sing 103
Anderson, Carl *156*
Anderson, Eddie 'Rochester' 115
Anderson, John Murray 35
Andrews, Julie 104, *106*(2), 139, 152
Annie 135, 141
Annie Get Your Gun 100, 135, 144
Anything Goes 143
April In Paris 98
Armstrong, Louis 139
Astaire, Adele 61
Astaire, Fred 12, 29, 30, 38, 49, *56*, 59(2), *60*(2), 61, *62*(2), 63(3), *63*, 64, 65(2), *66*, 67, 68, 69, 70, 78, 90, 100, *111*, *112*, 115, 120, *122*, 125, *127*, 135, 141
Astor, Mary *118*, 119
Austerlitz, Frederick (later Fred Astaire) 60
Avedon, Richard 29

B

Babes In Arms 52, 114
Babes On Broadway 52, 114
Bacon, Lloyd 41, 42
Baker, Carroll 85
Baker, Norma Jean (later Marilyn Monroe) 91
Ball, Lucille 38, 143
Band Wagon, The 58, 67, 68, 69, 111, 115, 120
Banton, Travis 12, 14, 16, 29, 84, 87(2)
Barkleys Of Broadway, The 65, 67, 127
Barrymore, John 22, 35
Barty, Billy 45
Bass, Saul 140
Baum, L. Frank 111
Baxter, Warner 42
Beals, Jennifer *81*
Beaton, Cecil 31, 137, 150, 151, 154
Beckett, Scotty *133*
Beckman, John 149
Becky Sharp 123
Belle Of New York, The 67, 127
Berkeley, Busby 38, 40, 41, 42, 45, 47, 48, 50, 55, 61, 90, 91, 114, 123
Berlin, Irving 61, 77, 92, 96
Berman, Pandro S. 61
Bernstein, Leonard 141
Best Foot Forward 143
Big Broadcast of 1938, The 27
Billy Rose's Diamond Horseshoe 90
Blackburn Twins, The *126*, 127
Blaine, Vivian *134*
Blonde Venus 83
Blondell, Joan *34*, 42, 47, 48
Blore, Eric 61
Blue Skies 65
Blyth, Ann 27, 28, 147

Boles, John *143*
Bolger, Ray *36*, 78
Born To Dance 77
Borodin, Alexander 147
Boy Friend, The 49
Brando, Marlon *140*
Brecht, Bertolt 157
Bremer, Lucille 65, 115, *118*, 119
Brice, Fanny 152
Brigadoon 146
Bright Eyes 87
Broadway 40, 135
Broadway Babies 135
Broadway Melody, The 34, 135
Broadway Melody Of 1936 77
Broadway Melody Of 1938 77
Broadway Melody Of 1940 49, 65, 77, 135
Broadway Scandals 135
Brooks, Mel 47
Brown, Nacio Herb 34, 111, *113*, 124
Bruce, Virginia 38, 77
Bryant, Sally *155*
Brynner, Yul 148
Buchanan, Jack 14, 68, 120
Burke, Billie *112*
Burns, George 64
By The Light Of The Silvery Moon 98

C

Cabaret 80, 137, 143, 155, 157
Cabin In The Sky 115
Cabot, Sebastian *147*
Cagney, James 42, 46, 78, 98
Calamity Jane 98
Call Me Madam 139
Can't Help Singing 28
Can't Stop The Music 80
Canova, Judy 100
Cansino, Rita 65
Cantor, Eddie 36, 38, 40(2), *41*, 87
Carefree 62(2)
Carlisle, Kitty 49
Caron, Leslie 12, 31, 69, *69*, 76, *120*
Carousel 148
Carroll, Joan *118*
Carson, Jack 98
Castle, Irene 57, 63
Castle, Vernon 58
Champion, Gower 79
Champion, Marge 79
Channing, Carol *107*, 139
Chaplin, Charlie 87
Chaplin, Saul 120
Charisse, Cyd 12, *67*, 68, 69, 76, 77, *111*(2), 115, *121*, *122*, 123, 147
Chevalier, Maurice 11, *12*, *13*, 14(2), *16*(2), *18*, *19*, 31, 35, 49
Churchill, Sarah 125
Clark, Carroll 61
Coburn, Charles 92
Cohan, George M. 78
Cohn, Harry 26
Colbert, Claudette 14
Colette 31
Comden, Betty 120, 125
Condos Brothers, The *90*
Connolly, Bobby 49, 65
Countess Of Monte Cristo, The 89
Cover Girl 70, 104
Coyne, Jeannie 146
Crain, Jeanne 29
Crawford, Joan 34, *35*, 57, 59(2)
Crayne, Dani *96*
Croce, Arlene 22
Crosby, Bing 20, 103, 127, 143
Cukor, George 16, 30, 113, 130, 131, 137
Curly Top 87
Curtis, Tony 96

D

Daddy Long Legs 69
Dailey, Dan 69, 78, 90, *124*, 125
Daley, Cass 100
Dames 42, 45
Damn Yankees 80, 138, 149
Damone, Vic 147
Damsel In Distress, A 64
Dancing Lady 49, 58, 61
Dandridge, Dorothy *140*, 141
Dangerous When Wet 127
Daniels, Bebe *143*
Daniels, William 21
Darling Lili 106
Darrieux, Danielle 29
Daughter Of Rosie O'Grady, The 91
Davenport, Harry *118*
Davies, Marion *26*, 34, *35*
Day, Doris 78, 98(2), *99*(2), 141
de Givenchy, Hubert 29
del Rio, Dolores *61*
DeMille, Cecil B. 35
Demy, Jacques 107
Deneuve, Catherine *107*
Desert Song, The *143*
Dietrich, Marlene 27, 83, *84*, 87, 106
Dior, Christian 29
Disney, Walt 27
Dixon, Lee *48*, 49
Dolly Sisters, The 90
Donen, Stanley 30, 50, 123, 124, 125(3), 138
Doren, Mamie Van *96*
Dorléac, Françoise *107*
Dorsey, Tommy *113*
Dotrice, Karen *106*
Down Argentine Way 89, 90
Down To Earth 104
Dreier, Hans 12, 16
Du Barry Was A Lady 143
Du Bois, Raoul Pene 143
Dubin, Al 41
Durante, Jimmy *133*
Durbin, Deanna 27, *28*
Duvivier, Julian 26
Dyke, Dick Van *106*

E

Easter Parade 65, 77, 127
Easy To Love 55, 127
Ebb, Fred 157
Ebsen, Buddy 78
Eddy, Nelson 21(2), 22, 23, 27
Edens, Roger 114
Edwards, Cliff ('Ukelele Ike') 34, 35
Eisner, Lotte 22
Ellington, Duke 115
Ellis, Anita 104
Ellis, Antonia *155*
Emperor Waltz, The 20
Enos, William Berkeley (Busby Berkeley) 55
Enright, Ray 42
Etting, Ruth 98
Every Day's A Holiday 87
Ewell, Tom 88, 96

F

Fairbanks, Douglas Jr 20
Faith, Percy 98
Fame 80, *80*
Fantasia 27
Farrell, Glenda 42
Fashions Of 1934 45
Faye, Alice 87, 88(2), 89, *90*
Fejos, Paul 40
Finian's Rainbow 69, 141
Firefly, The 23
Flagstad, Kirsten 27

Flashdance 80, 81
Fleet's In, The 103
Fleming, Victor 113
Flirtation Walk 49
Flying Down To Rio 49, 61
Folies Bergere 49
Follow The Fleet 62, 63
Folsey, George 119
Fontaine, Joan 20, 64, *64*
Footlight Parade 42, 45(2), 46
For Me And My Gal 70
Forbstein, Leo 41
42nd Street 45, 46, 50
Fosse, Bob 79, 80, 136, 137, 141, *143*, 146, 155(2)
Francis, Connie 97
Frank, Anne 28
Freed, Arthur 34, 65, 66, 109, 111, *112*, 113, 114, 119, 123, 124, 127, 144
French Line, The 102
Froman, Jane 103
Funny Face 29, 69
Funny Girl 38, 138, 152

G

Gable, Clark 59, *110*
Gang's All Here, The 54, 91
Garber, Matthew *106*
Garbo, Greta 19
Gardner, Ava 98, 123, *138*
Garland, Judy 38(2), 50, *51*, *56*, 65, 70, 100, *108*, 110(2), 111, *112*, 113, *114*, 115, *118*(3), 119(2), 120, 125, 126, *127*, 130(2), *131*(2), 132, 133, 155
Garrett, Betty 123
Garson, Greer 119
Gay Divorcee, The 61, 63, 89
Gaynor, Mitzi *92*, *103*, *137*, 139
Gentlemen Marry Brunettes 29
Gentlemen Prefer Blondes *92*, 102
George White's Scandals 77
Gershwin, George 61, 120
Gibbons, Cedric 18, 21, 23
Gigi 31, 150
Gilbert, John *18*
Gilda 104
Girl Can't Help It, The 96
Girl Crazy 114
Girl Of The Golden West, The 22
Give A Girl A Break 79
Glorifying The American Girl 36
Go Into Your Dance 49
Goddard, Paulette 65
Goin' To Town 84
Gold Diggers In Paris 48
Gold Diggers Of 1933 42, 45, 47
Gold Diggers Of 1935 42, 46
Gold Diggers Of 1937 47
Gold Diggers Of Broadway 135
Goldwyn, Samuel 38, 140
Good News 126
Gould, Dave 36, 49
Grable, Betty 19, *20*, 40, 89, 90, 91, *91*, 92
Grace Moore Story, The 27
Grahame, Gloria 148
Gravet, Fernand 26
Gray, Dolores 125, 147
Gray, Joel 157
Grayson, Kathryn 10, *27*(2), *28*, 29, 38, 77, 108, *119*, *133*, *146*
Grease 157
Great Caruso, The 28
Great Waltz, The 23
Great Ziegfeld, The 36
Green, Adolph 120, 125
Greenburg, Gilbert Adrian (Adrian) 19
Greene, Graham 60
Greenwood, Charlotte 78
Grey, Joel *156*

Grossman, Arthur (later Arthur Freed) 111
Grot, Anton 41
Guilaroff, Sydney 18, *85*
Guinan, Texas 100
Guys And Dolls 136
Gypsy 138, 139, 149, 157

H

Hagen, Jean 124
Hair 157
Hale, Georgina *155*
Hall, Jon 144
Hallejulah I'm A Bum 47
Hammerstein, Oscar II 135, 137, 147
Haney, Carol 146
Happy Go Lucky 100
Harkrider, John 40
Harlow, Jean 83(2), *85*
Harris, Phil 88
Harris, Richard *152*
Hart, Lorenz 141
Harvey Girls, The 110
Haver, June 91(2)
Hayward, Susan *103*
Hayworth, Rita *64*, 65, 70, 104(2), *105*(2), 141
Head, Edith 20, 29, 143
Hello, Dolly! 138, 154
Hello, Frisco, Hello 87
Henie, Sonja 88, 89, *89*
Hepburn, Audrey 29, 69, 150, *151*
Herbert, Hugh 42
Hers To Hold 28
High Society 127
His Butler's Sister 28
Holiday In Mexico 29
Hollywood Hotel 48
Hollywood Revue Of 1929 34, 58
Hope, Bob 27, 78, 102, *103*
Hope, Frederic 18
Hopkins, Miriam 14
Horne, Lena 38, 115
Horton, Edward Everett 61, 62, 67, 89
How To Marry A Millionaire 92
Hubert, Ali 19
Hubert, Rene 19
Hughes, Howard 102
Hunter, Tab 149
Huston, John 141
Hutton, Betty 100(2), 103, 144, *146*

I

I Married An Angel 22(2)
I Wonder Who's Kissing Her Now 91
I'll Get By 91
I'll See You In My Dreams 98
I'm No Angel 84
In Old Chicago 87
In The Good Old Summertime 132
Incendiary Blonde 100
Innocents In Paris 14
Irene 127
Irish Eyes Are Smiling 91
It's Always Fair Weather 69, 74, 76, 125
Iturbi, Jose 29, *29*

J

Jazz Singer, The 109
Jeanmaire, Zizi *58*
Jilliann, Ann 149
Johnson, Van 147
Jolson, Al 47, 49, 87, 109
Jones, Allan 23, 38
Jones, Shirley *137*, 147
Jourdan, Louis *31*
Jumbo 98
June, Ray 30
Jungle Princess, The 103
Just Around The Corner 87

K

Kael, Pauline 70
Kalloch, Robert 26
Kalmus, Dr Herbert 89

Kalmus, Natalie 89
Kander, John 157
Kauffmann, Stanley 31
Kaumeyer, Dorothy (later Lamour) 103
Kaye, Danny 40, 100, *100*
Keaton, Buster 34, *35*
Keel, Howard 77, 100, *108*, 125, 144, 146, 147
Keeler, Ruby *32*, 42(2), 45(2), 46(2), *48*, 49(3), 64
Kelly, Gene 12, 38, 65, 69, 70(2), 74, *75*, 76, 78, 79, 110, *111*, 115, 120(2), 123, 124, 125, 138(2), *139*, 147
Kelly, Grace 127, *127*
Kern, Jerome 61, 62, 65, 119(2), 143
Kerr, Deborah *148*, 149
Kibbee, Guy 42
Kid From Spain, The 40
Kidd, Michael 50, 69, 122, *124*, 125(2), 126, 138
King, Alexander 106
King And I, The 148
King, Charles *34*
King Of Jazz 35
King Steps Out, The 27
Kismet 146, 147
Kiss Me Kate 78, 79, 138, 146
Klondike Annie 84
Knight, Fuzzy *138*
Korjus, Miliza 26

L

Lady In The Dark 143
Lady's Morals, A 26
Lamarr, Hedy 38, *38*
Lamas, Fernando 20
Lamour, Dorothy 103
Lang, Walter 149
Lanza, Mario *10*, 28
Laurie, Piper *96*
Lawford, Peter 125, 127, *133*
Lawrence, Gertrude 106
Lee, Gypsy Rose *150*
Lee, Sammy 49
Leisen, Mitchell 49, 143
Lemmon, Jack 96
Leonard, Robert Z. 21, 23
Lerner, Alan Jay 120, 123, 125
LeRoy, Mervyn 42, 47, 111, 149
Les Girls 30
Lester, Mark *141*
LeSueur, Lucille (later Joan Crawford) 58
Let's Dance 100
Let's Make Love 96
Levant, Oscar *98*, 111
Lightner, Winnie *35*
Lillian Russell 87
Lillie, Bea 35
Lind, Jenny 26
Liszt, Franz 28
Little, Caryl *155*
Little Miss Broadway 87
Little Miss Marker 87
Little Night Music, A 157
Lloyd-Webber, Andrew 156
Logan, Joshua 137(2)
Lombard, Carole 58
Loos, Anita 83, 92
Lord Byron Of Broadway 135
Louis, Jean 104, 105
Love, Bessie 34, *34*
Love Happy 91
Love Me Or Leave Me 98
Love Me Tonight 16, 123
Love Parade, The 14(2), 31
Lovely To Look At 29
Loy, Myrna 16, 35
Lubitsch, Ernst 12, 19, 20, 31, 35
Lullaby Of Broadway 98
Lulu Belle 103
Luxury Liner 29

M

MacDonald, Jeanette 11, *13*(2), 14, *14*(2), 16, 18, *18*, 21, *21*(2), 22, 22, 23, 27, 29, 31
MacDonald, Ray *126*, (2), 127

MacLaine, Shirley *136*, 137
MacMurray, Fred 91
MacRae, Gordon 98, 147
Madam Satan 35
Maire, Charles Le 19
Make Mine Music 27
Mamoulian, Rouben 16, 89, 122, 123
Mankiewicz, Joseph 136
Mansfield, Jayne 96, *97*(2)
Marsh, Oliver T. 18, 21, 23
Martin, Mary 139(2)
Martin, Steve 50, *50*
Marx, Groucho 91, 98
Marx Brothers, The 111
Mary Poppins 106, 152
Mason, James 130, *131*, 132
Matthews, Jessie 64
Mattox, Matt 125
Maxwell, Marilyn *122*, 123
Mayer, Louis B. 22, 77, 111, 114, 119
Mayo, Archie 42
Mayo, Virginia 78, 100
Maytime 22(2), 27
Mazurki, Mike *147*
McCracken, Joan *126*
Meet Me In St Louis 98, 110, 119, 126, 132
Melchior, Lauritz 27, 28
Mendelssohn, Felix 28
Merkel, Una *32*, 42, 45
Merman, Ethel 139, 143
Merry Widow, The 11, 18
Merry Widow (1952), The 20
Michael, Gertrude 49
Midler, Bette 157
Mille, Agnes De *137*
Miller, Ann 54, 55, 77(2), 79, 123, 146(2)
Miller, Marilyn 143
Million Dollar Mermaid 55
Milner, Victor 12, 16
Minnelli, Liza 119, 120, 139, 155, 157
Minnelli, Vincente 114, *115*(2), 119(2), 120, 123, 146, 147, 154(2), 155
Miranda, Carmen *53*, 54(2)
Misfits, The 96
Mitchell, Cameron *148*
Mitchell, Millard 111
Monkey Business 92
Monroe, Marilyn 78, *82*, 83, 91, *92*(3), 96, 100, 106
Montalban, Ricardo *133*
Monte Carlo 11, 14
Moody, Ron *141*
Moon Over Miami 90, 91
Moore, Grace 18, 26
Moreno, Rita *148*
Morgan, Dennis 38, *98*
Morgan, Helen 36
Morocco 106
Mother Wore Tights 90
Movie Movie 50
Munshin, Jules 69, 78, 123
Murder At The Vanities 49
Murphy, George 77, 135
Murray, Mae *18*
My Fair Lady 137, 150
My Gal Sal 104
My Lucky Star 88

N

Naish, J. Carrol *146*
Naughty Marietta 22
Negri, Pola *14*
Nelson, Gene 78
New Moon 22
Newman, Bernard 29, 61, 63
Niagara 92
Nicholas Brothers, The 69, 79
Nordstrom, Clarence 45
North, Sheree *82*
Novarro, Ramon *14*

O

O'Brien, Margaret 119
O'Brien, Virginia 38
O'Connor, Donald 69, *70*, 78, *92*, 96, 124

O'Hara, John 141
O'Neill, Eugene 122, 123
Oh, You Beautiful Doll 91
Oklahoma! 137, 147
On A Clear Day You Can See Forever 154
On Moonlight Bay 98
On The Avenue 87
On The Town 69, 76, 78, 109, 110, 123, 125
One Hour With You 16
One Hundred Men And A Girl, 28
One In A Million 88
One Night Of Love 26
Orry-Kelly 41, 90, 147
Our Blushing Brides 58
Our Dancing Daughters 58
Outlaw, The 102

P

Page, Anita 34
Paget, Debra *102*
Painting The Clouds With Sunshine 100
Pajama Game, The 80, 138, 141
Pal Joey 141
Paleface, The 102
Palmy Days 40
Pan, Hermes 61, 67, *104*, 146
Pangborn, Franklin 61
Paramount On Parade 35
Parton, Dolly 157
Pasternak, Joe 27, 28, 130
Payne, John 87, 88
Pennies From Heaven 50
Perils Of Pauline, The 100
Peters, Bernadette *50*
Petit, Roland 76
Pin Up Girl 90
Pirate, The 69, 74, 79, 110, 120
Plunkett, Walter 28, 64, 124
Poitier, Sidney 141
Polglase, Van Nest 61, 64, 65
Polito, Sol 41
Pons, Lily 27
Porgy And Bess 141
Porter, Cole 23, 61, 74, 120, 143(2), 146
Powell, Dick 42(3), 45(2), 46, 47, 49(2), 50
Powell, Eleanor 23, *64*, 65, 77(2)
Powell, Jane 27, 28, 29(2), 125(2), *133*
Powell, William 36, *37*, 38
Power, Tyrone 87, 88
Preminger, Otto 19, 96, 140, 141
Prince, Harold 157
Prinz, Eddie 49
Producers, The 47
Prowse, Juliet *149*
Purdom, Edmund 28

Q

Quinn, Aileen *141*

R

Raft, George 58
Rainer, Luise 26
Raitt, John 141
Rall, Tommy 79, 146
Randell, Ron 77
Raphaelson, Samson 16, 18
Rasch, Albertina 22, 23, 34
Raye, Martha 100
Ready, Willing And Able 49
Reagan, Ronald 100
Reckless 35
Reed, Carol 141
Rettig, Tommy 96
Reynolds, Debbie 79, 124
Rice, Tim 156
Rich, Young and Pretty 29
Richards, Jeff 125
Riefenstahl, Leni 47
Rin-Tin-Tin 35
Rio Rita 143
River Of No Return 96
Robbins, Jerome 136, 149
Roberta 29, 63
Roberti, Lyda *40*
Robinson, Bill 'Bojangles' 62, 79

Rodgers, Richard 135, 137, 147
Rodgers and Hart 126
Rogers, Ginger 32, 45, 47, 60, 61(2), 62, 63(3), 64, 65, 66, 87, 112, 143, 144
Rogers, Roy 103
Roman Scandals 40
Romberg, Sigmund 133
Romeo And Juliet 23
Rooney, Mickey 50, 51(2), 52, 54, 111, 113, 114, 122, 123, 126
Rosalie 23
Rose, David 119
Rose, Helen 20, 58, 98, 125, 127
Rose Marie 22(2)
Rose Of Washington Square 87
Royal Wedding 67, 125
Royce, Betty 124
Runkle, Theadora Van 157
Runyon, Damon 87, 136
Russell, Jane 29, 92, 102
Russell, Ken 49, 155
Russell, Rosalind 139, 149, 150
Ruttenberg, Joseph 28

S

Sally 143
Salome 104
San Francisco 27
Sanders, George 91
Sandrich, Mark 61, 65
Sarris, Andrew 19
Saturday Night Fever 80
Scheider, Roy 80
Schiaparelli 87
Second Chorus 65
Selznick, David O. 60
Seven Brides For Seven Brothers 29, 79, 125
Seven Little Foys, The 78
Seven Year Itch, The 106
Shall We Dance 62, 63, 66
Sharaff, Irene 119, 120, 141, 149, 154
Shaw, Wini 46
She Done Him Wrong 84
She's Working Her Way Through College 100
Shearer, Douglas 21
Shocking Miss Pilgrim, The 90
Show Boat 98, 137
Show Of Shows, The 35
Sidney, George 110, 144, 146
Silk Stockings 12, 67, 68
Silvers, Phil 70
Simmons, Jean 140
Sinatra, Frank 69, 74, 123, 123, 130, 141, 148
Singin' In The Rain 69, 74, 77, 78, 110, 124
Slightly French 103
Small Town Girl 54, 79
Smiling Lieutenant, The 14
Smith, Oliver 147
Snow, Carmel 30
So This Is Love 27
Some Like It Hot 96
Son Of Paleface 102
Sondheim, Stephen 141, 157
Song Is Born, A 100
Sothern, Ann 32, 35
Sound Of Music, The 106, 137, 139, 152
South Pacific 137, 139, 141
Stand Up And Cheer 87
Star! 106
Star Is Born, A 130, 132
State Fair 88
Staying Alive 80, 81
Steiger, Rod 147, 148
Stewart, Donald Ogden 47
Stokowski, Leopold 27, 28
Stork Club, The 100
Stormy Weather 79
Story Of Vernon And Irene Castle, The 63
Stowaway 87
Stradling, Harry 149
Straus, Oscar 16
Strauss, Johann 23
Streisand, Barbra 38, 134, 139(2), 152, 153, 154, 157
Strike Up The Band 52, 114
Stromberg, Hunt 21

Stuart, Gloria 42
Student Prince, The 28
Sullivan, Jerri 100
Summer Holiday 123, 126
Summer Stock 74, 130
Sun Valley Serenade 88
Sunny 143
Sunny Side Up 35
Swarthout, Gladys 26
Sweet Charity 80, 137
Sweet Rosie O'Grady 90
Sweethearts 22(2)
Swing Time 62, 63(2)

T

Take Me Out To The Ballgame 74, 123
Tashlin, Frank 96, 97
Taylor, Elizabeth 157
Tchaikovsky, Peter Ilyitch 27
Tea For Two 98
Temple, Shirley 79, 87(2), 113
That Lady In Ermine 19
That Midnight Kiss 28
That Night In Rio 87
There's No Business Like Show Business 92, 96
Thompson, Kay 30
Thoroughly Modern Millie 106
Thousands Cheer 28, 70
Three Daring Daughters 29
Three Little Girls In Blue 91
Three Musketeers, The 70
Three Smart Girls 28
Three Smart Girls Grow Up 28
Thrill Of Romance 27
Till The Clouds Roll By 119, 127
Tin Pan Alley 87, 91
Tip, Tap and Toe 79
Toast of New Orleans, The 28
Tobin, Genevieve 16
Tone, Franchot 58
Tonight And Every Night 104
Too Hot To Handle 96
Top Hat 61, 63(2), 67
Torch Song 58
Travilla, William 92(2)
Travolta, John 80(2), 81, 157
Tree, Dolly 23
Triumph Of The Will, The 47
Truscott, John 152
Turner, Lana 10, 20, 34, 38
Two Sisters From Boston 28
Tyler, Parker 27

U

Up In Arms 40

V

Vajda, Ernest 18
Valentino, Rudolph 14
Vallee, Rudy 36
Van, Bobby 79, 146
Van Dyke, W.S. 21, 22
Vera-Ellen 67, 68, 76, 123
Verdi, Guiseppe 29
Verdon, Gwen 139, 149, 149
Victor-Victoria 106
Von Sternberg, Joseph 27

W

Wakeling, Gwen 88, 104
Wallace, Paul 150
Wallis, Shani 141
Walston, Ray 149
Walters, Charles 66, 126, 127(2)
Warner, Jack 150
Warren, Harry 41
Warren, Leslie Anne 106
Waters, Ethel 115
Weekend In Havana 88
Weill, Kurt 157
West, Mae 84(2), 86(2)
West, Vera 28

West Side Story 136, 141
Whirl Of Life, The 57
White, Pearl 100
Whitmore, James 146
Whoopee! 38, 40
Wilder, Billy 20, 91
Wilding, Michael 58
Williams, Esther 27, 38, 45, 55, 123, 127, 132, 133
Wilson, Sandy 49
Wing, Toby 50
Wintertime 89
Wizard Of Oz, The 49, 111, 113, 130
Wonder Man 100
Wood, Natalie 149, 150(2)
Wood, Yvonne 54
Words And Music 76, 127
Wynn, Keenan 146

Y

Yankee Doodle Dandy 78
Yolanda And The Thief 65, 115, 120
You Were Never Lovelier 65
You'll Never Get Rich 65
Young, Loretta 35
Young, Robert 87

Z

Zanuck, Darryl F. 41, 88
Ziegfeld, Florenz 33, 36, 38
Ziegfeld Follies 38, 65, 70, 119, 120
Ziegfeld Girl 38
Zucco, George 23

Acknowledgements

The feature articles which appear in each chapter were devised and written by **Tom Hutchinson**.

The author wishes to thank his irreplaceable editor, Robyn Karney, for her expertise, constructive criticism and encouragement. Also Gilbert Adair, Clive Hirschhorn and Tom Vallance, all of whom allowed me to draw from their fund of knowledge.

Additional thanks to:
Michaela Frey
Anello & Davide
Nicola Keen and Elizabeth Gilbert
Reg Sutton of Samuelsons

The publishers wish to thank the following individuals and organisations for their kind permission to reproduce the pictures in this book:

BBC Hulton Picture Library 128 above inset, 129 above and centre; Joel Finler 11, 12, 13 inset, 14–22, 23 above, 24 inset above and below left, 26–34, 36 below, 37–39, 40 below, 41 below, 42 above and below, 43 top right and centre, 44 above, 45–48, 50 above, 53–59, 60 above, 61 below, 62 above, 63–65, 66 below, 67 above and below, 69 below, 70–71, 74 right, 75 below, 76 below, 77–79, 80 below, 81 above, 83 right, 84–88, 90–93, 95 below right, 96–100, 102, 103 above, 103 below left, 104–107, 109, 110 below, 111–112, 114, 115 above, 116 above, and below right, 117 centre and right, 118, 119 above, 120 above and below, 124 above, 125, 127 right, 128 below inset, 130 left and right, 132 above and below, 133 left and right, 135 right, 136 above and below, 137 below, 138 below, 139, 141–143, 146 below, 147 above and below, 148 below, 149 above and below, 150 left, 151–157; The Kobal Collection 10–11, 13, 24, 25 right, 35, 36 above, 40 above, 41 above, 43 below left, 44 below, 49, 50 below, 51, 52, 60 below, 61 above, 62 below, 66 above, 69 above, 72, 73, 74 left, 75 above, 76 above, 80 above, 81 below right, 82–83, 89,
94, 95 above, and below left, above right, 101, 103 below left, 108–109, 110 below, 113, 115 below, 116 below left, 117 left, 118 below right, 119 below, 121, 122, 123, 124 below, 126, 127 left, 131, 134–135, 137 above left and right, 138 above, 140 144, 146 above, 148 above, 150 above and below right; National Film Archive 68, 81 below left, 128, 129 below; Topham Picture Library 145

Special photography by Simon de Courcy Wheeler 1, 2–3, 4–5, 8–9

Permissions Acknowledgements

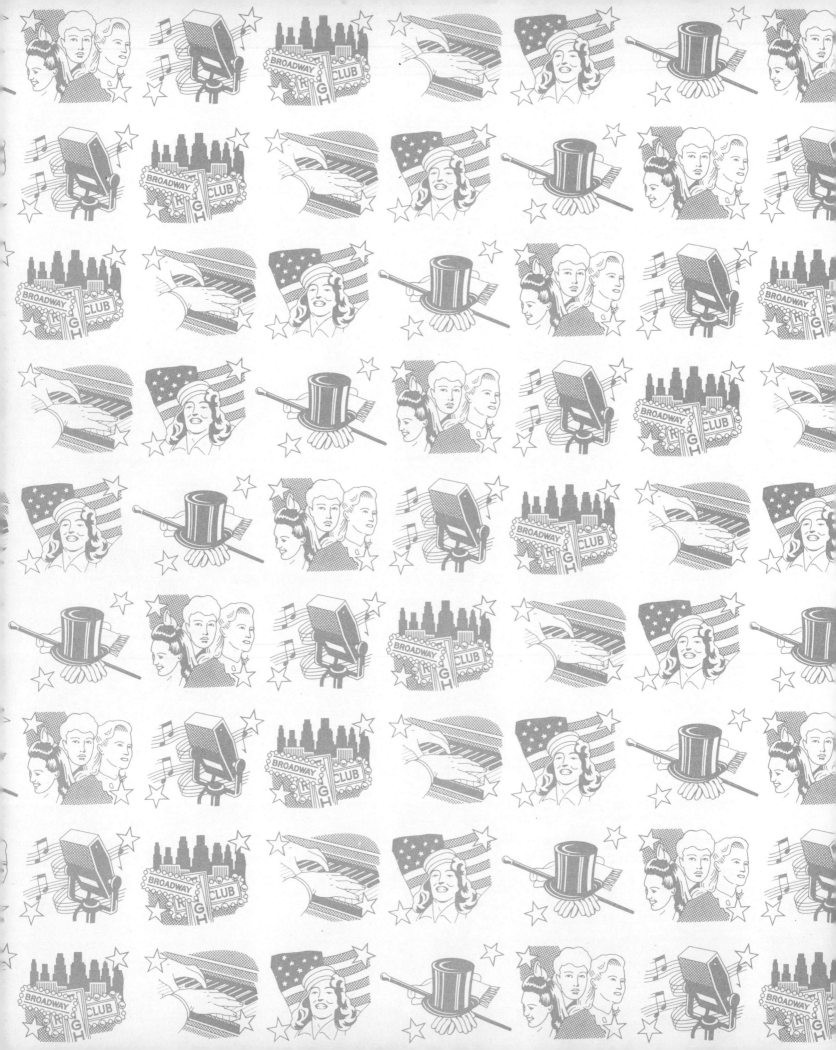